W9-DCO-011

8.00

RELIGIOUS CUSTOMS
IN THE FAMILY

RELIGIOUS CUSTOMS
IN THE FAMILY

THE RADIATION OF THE LITURGY INTO CATHOLIC HOMES

By Fr. Francis X. Weiser, S.J.

"This is the day which the Lord hath made: let us be glad and rejoice therein." —Psalms 117:24

TAN BOOKS AND PUBLISHERS, INC.
Rockford, Illinois 61105

Imprimi potest: James E. Coleran, S.J.
Provincial
Boston
October 20, 1956

Nihil obstat: John Eidenschink, O.S.B., J.C.D.
Censor deputatus

Imprimatur: ✚ Peter W. Bartholome, D.D.
Bishop of St. Cloud
October 7, 1956

Copyright © 1956 by The Order of St. Benedict, Inc., Collegeville, Minn. Retypeset and republished in 1998 by TAN Books and Publishers, Inc. The type in this book is the property of TAN Books and Publishers and may not be reproduced without written permission from the Publisher, except that brief selections may be copied without permission, giving credit. (This restriction refers only to this *type,* not to quotations from the book.)

ISBN: 0-89555-613-8

Library of Congress Catalog No.: 97-62522

Printed and bound in the United States of America.

TAN BOOKS AND PUBLISHERS, INC.
P.O. Box 424
Rockford, Illinois 61105
1998

"Why doth one day excel another, and one light another, and one year another year, when all come of the sun? By the knowledge of the Lord they were distinguished, the sun being made, and keeping his commandment. And he ordered the seasons, and holidays of them, and in them they celebrated festivals at an hour. Some of them God made high and great days, and some of them he put in the number of ordinary days."

—*Ecclesiasticus* 33:7-10

CONTENTS

RELIGIOUS CUSTOMS
IN THE FAMILY

"O God, Who dost give us joy by the yearly solemnity of Our Lord's Resurrection, mercifully grant that we who celebrate this temporal feast may deserve to attain everlasting happiness. Through the same Christ Our Lord. Amen."

—Collect for Easter Wednesday
The Roman Missal

—Part One—
GENERAL CUSTOMS

–1–

THE HOLY SACRIFICE

From the very beginnings of Christianity, the Church has given a special priority and attention to Holy Mass over all other services because it is the one and only Sacrifice of the New Testament. In fact, in the Mass as the center and soul of liturgy, Christ offers Himself daily anew for each one of us. It is the infinite and immaculate oblation, the highest act of worship we can perform. Not the priest alone offers this Sacrifice, but with him all the faithful who attend, thus exercising the "royal priesthood" which St. Peter attributes to them. There is no greater action you could ever perform in your life than this co-operation in offering the Holy Sacrifice to the heavenly Father.

The fruit of Christ's Redemption and sanctification is poured into our hearts through this Sacrifice. In Communion He unites Himself with us most intimately and nourishes our souls with supernatural love and grace. In addition, every Communion casts into our bodies the "seed of eternal glory" according to the Saviour's own word, "He that eateth my flesh, and drinketh my blood, hath everlasting life: and I will raise him up in the last day." (*John* 6:55).

The faithful, on their part, have at all times gladly and gratefully followed the command of the Church to assist at the Holy Sacrifice on Sundays and prescribed holydays. Sincere Catholics have always considered it a privilege rather than a duty to observe this law.

In the course of centuries, people also developed various customs in their families which helped them to give due honor and attention to the Holy Sacrifice and to draw greater fruit from it.

There is the ancient practice of preparing the soul by prayer while going to Mass. Instead of chatting, the members of the family pray together, or each one prays in silence by himself, on their way to church. This custom is of special value in the religious education of smaller children. It makes them realize, without many words of explanation, how great and holy the Sacrifice of the Mass must be.

Another custom practiced in many families is a short reading of the Sunday Mass prayers on the previous evening at home, to fill the soul with the sublime thoughts and inspirations contained in the liturgical texts. For children this may best be done by one of the parents, and a simple explanation might be given. Boys and girls of high school age should have their own missals and be familiar with their use.

It was a widespread custom years ago that older children would go to Mass at least once a week besides Sunday, to represent the family before the altar of God, even when it was not a matter of strict obligation. Today, so many parents do not even seem to consider such a possibility. Surely the children are not overburdened with tasks of duty every night that they must of necessity sleep late every morning of the week? There are still families, thank God, whose children are prudently inspired and guided by their parents and will cheerfully get up in the morning to attend Mass on a weekday once in awhile.

In many localities it is customary to ring the church bells at the beginning of every Mass and at the Consecration. Thus, everyone in the town or village can follow the Holy Sacrifice. At the sound of the Consecration bell, the faithful stop their work for a minute, cross themselves, say a short prayer and adore Our Lord, who has just again become present on their altar, re-enacting His Sacrifice. In places where bells are not generally rung, it might be suggested that parents and children include themselves in the Holy Masses of their parish church every day at the Morning Offering, to obtain the grace and blessing of Heaven, at least by a spiritual union with the Sacrifice of Christ.

Finally, there is the holy and pious custom of having Masses offered for various intentions, especially for the repose of the souls of departed relatives and friends. The stipend given on such occasions is not a "paying" for the Mass, of course, but a donation which we present as a small sacrifice on our part, to symbolize our gratitude for the overwhelming benefit of having the divine Sacrifice offered for our intentions and needs.

Sometimes the question is asked, "How about people who are so poor that they cannot afford the Mass stipend?" The answer, first of all, is that they share in every Mass offered by their pastor. Then too, the Church has not forgotten the poor in her arrangements and laws. In order not to embarrass them by having to ask for Masses without being able to give the donation, she has prescribed centuries ago that every parish priest must offer the Holy Sacrifice for his parishioners on every Sunday and on holydays (including the abrogated holydays) *without any stipend*. This law still obliges every parish priest in the whole world. (*Codex Juris Canonici* [1917], Can. 306, 339, 466.)

It might be suggested to many Catholic parents that the Holy Sacrifice will most surely procure for them the necessary graces and helps in all the duties of parenthood and married life. I know a father and mother who came to the rectory every week without fail, asking that a Mass be offered during the week for God's special help in bringing up their five children. Whenever possible, one of them attended this Mass with two or three of their children. These youngsters are all grown up now. The parents managed to send them all to Catholic colleges. One is a priest, one a nun, one is studying for the priesthood, and the other two are happily married and raising fine Catholic families of their own.

THE HOLY EUCHARIST

Reverence and love toward this great Sacrament have caused from ancient times the custom in Catholic families that every member should pay a daily visit to Our Lord in the Tabernacle. In our modern times, when people often live a great distance from the church or rush through the town in cars, this custom presents more difficulties than in the past. In many cases, however, it could be practiced without much inconvenience, if only parents would train their children from the first year of grammar school to drop into a nearby church and visit Our Lord for a few moments. This inspiration should not be left to the nuns of the Catholic school. When the good sister suggests such a visit, your child should be able to say, "That's what Daddy and Mother have told me, and what I am already doing."

In a similar way, the practice of making a proper thanksgiving after Holy Communion should be impressed on children from the beginning. Too many people leave church right at the close of Mass without devoting sufficient time to the prayerful union with Christ after having received Him. These fifteen minutes following the reception of the Holy Eucharist are the most precious time of prayer we have.

A custom which has been spreading of late—and God grant that it may soon become general—is the practice that on First Communion day parents receive the Holy Eucharist together with their child. In parishes where this custom is already established, experience has shown that fathers and mothers who have been away from the Sacraments for many years will readily resume the practice of their faith, in order to accompany their little ones to the Communion rail on this wonderful occasion.

One unfortunate "custom" which I have encountered frequently in my priestly experience is the idea implanted into little children that it would be terribly wrong and even sinful if they ever touched the Sacred Host with their teeth while receiving Communion. This erroneous conviction has caused many children to be frightened when they approach the Holy Eucharist. Actually, the Apostles on Holy Thursday chewed and ate the Holy Sacrament in the natural way. The Church has never declared that the use of the teeth is sinful or wrong. Many priests chew the large Host in Holy Communion, eating it just as the Apostles did.

It is true, we do not usually chew the small Host. The reason, however, is not that it would be sinful, but that it is not necessary. Parents and nuns should explain this to the children and assure them that it is perfectly all right if for some reason they should hold or touch the Host with their teeth.

−2−

THE SACRAMENTS

Many and varied are the customs that have been practiced from ancient times in connection with the Holy Sacraments of the Church. We mention here only those which may be of special help and significance for the Christian families of today.

BAPTISM

It was a widespread practice among Catholic populations—and still is today in many places—that the parents themselves provide the candle which the priest will use in the ceremony of Baptism. According to the *Ritual*, this candle is lit and handed to the sponsor to hold while the priest addresses the following words to the child: "Receive this lighted candle, and keep your Baptism above reproach. Keep the Commandments of God, so that when the Lord comes to His marriage feast, you may meet Him in the halls of Heaven with all His Saints, and may live with Him forever. Amen."

It certainly is in keeping with the spirit of the liturgy of Baptism for the baptized person to retain this candle as a cherished symbol of his spiritual birth. These baptismal candles are often decorated with religious designs. The priest will gladly use such a candle, if brought by the parents, and allow them to take it home after the ceremony, according to the pious custom of many centuries.

The baptismal candle is then carefully kept in the home. Every year, on the anniversary of Baptism, it is lit for a few minutes while the child in joyful prayer thanks God for the grace of the Sacrament and renews the baptismal vows. In many places it is customary to use the baptismal candle on solemn occasions in later life: on the day of First Holy Communion; on one's Wedding Day; while receiving the Sacraments in serious illness; and especially at the hour of death. Afterwards, what is left of the candle is put at the head of the coffin during the wake and kept burning until it is consumed.

Parents who already have children of school age would do well to take them along to church for the Baptism of a little brother or sister. They might ask the priest to give a short explanation of the holy rite; or, if this should not be possible, father or mother could explain the prayers and ceremonies at home before Baptism. Thus, the children will follow with interest and devotion and will better understand the great meaning and importance of their own Baptism. An occasion like this is one of the most valuable means of religious instruction. Here the children are taught not only in words, but through the actual performance of the holy liturgy with all its light, warmth and grace.

In many places the anniversary of Baptism is joyfully kept as a personal feast day, as the true birthday of supernatural life. People observe it by attending Mass, receiving Communion, renewing their baptismal vows, burning the candle of Baptism for a little while and performing some other acts of devotion during the day. A visit to the parish baptistry would be most appropriate. Very often, however, the memory of Baptism is rather combined with the celebration of the Saint's day whose name was received at the Christening (see the chapter, "The Name Day," p. 26).

PENANCE

In His great love and kindness, Our Lord has made Confession so simple and easy for us that many people, especially children, pay little attention to a devout and careful preparation. How often does one see youngsters rush into a church from their play and games in the street, hardly genuflect and dive into the confessional, still out of breath from running! Parents should train their children to spend a few minutes in sincere and serious prayer before they enter the tribunal of mercy. Likewise, after the Sacrament, they should be taught to make a devout thanksgiving.

An old and very wholesome practice demanded that children, before going to Confession, should ask forgiveness from their parents for offenses and faults committed in the home. This can be done very simply, although in true sincerity. It impresses upon their minds the fact that the parents are God's representatives; it also helps them to better fight their faults in the future. This custom prevailed in our home when I was a little boy. Before going to Confession, I would come to Mother and say, "Please forgive me, Mother; I am sorry for everything." She would then make the Sign of the Cross on my forehead and answer, "Father and I forgive you, and God will forgive you, too. Make a good Confession, and God bless you!" How clean, warm and happy did I feel after these Confessions!

Such customs not only deepen the religious life of the child, but also exert a powerful preventive influence. By asking forgiveness from the parents without having to mention his individual faults, the child comes to realize that sincerity and contrition are the main requisites for a good Confession, not the frightening task of discovering and mentioning every little detail that possibly might be a sin. Thus, a custom like the above is a simple and effective means of training the children's conscience away from unreasonable scruples and developing a correct, helpful attitude toward Confession.

CONFIRMATION

According to the ancient custom, the day of Confirmation, like First Communion day, is kept as a true holyday in the Christian family. As far as possible, parents, brothers and sisters celebrate it with the child who has been confirmed. The whole day's program breathes a spirit of solemnity, joy and devotion. Little presents (missal, prayer book or other religious objects) help to keep the day in joyful memory. In the evening, parents and child once more go to church to attend a service of devotion or to make a private visit in thanksgiving for the Sacrament.

EXTREME UNCTION

For sincere Catholics, it is not only a custom *but a sacred duty* to call a priest as soon as a member of the family is seriously ill and eventual death might be a possible consequence. Since this holy Sacrament is intended not only to forgive sins, but also to strengthen the powers of body and soul it would be foolish and almost cruel on the part of relatives to wait until death is imminent. How many persons have regained their health through the grace of this Sacrament because it was administered to them in good time!

One often hears the fear mentioned that Extreme Unction would scare the sick person and do him harm. People who express such fear only show their ignorance and are in great need of proper instruction. Actually, this Sacrament confers such a relief upon the mind, body and soul of the patient that calling the priest to anoint him is the very help he needs, in addition to medical care.

If Extreme Unction is administered in the home, the family should prepare a table covered with linen and carrying the following items: a crucifix and two candles, holy water, a glass with ordinary water, a small spoon, a bowl or saucer with some pieces of soft bread and a little heap of salt (for the priest to wipe the holy oil from his fingers), a small towel, and some little wads of cotton. Next to the table might be put a small basin of water, so the priest can wash his hands after the ceremony.

When the priest comes to the house with the Blessed Sacrament, one member of the family should precede him into the sick-room, bearing a lighted candle. [The others should kneel as the Blessed Sacrament passes by.] It sometimes happens that people leave the priest entirely alone with the sick person from beginning to end. This should not be. Apart from Confession, the members of the family should devoutly attend the sacred rites, kneeling or standing in the room and following the *Ritual* prayers while the priest administers the Sacraments and blessings.

MATRIMONY

The customary phrase, "married by the priest," is inaccurate. For it is not the priest who administers the Sacrament of Matrimony to the couple; they give it to each other when they pronounce the words of consent: *I will*. The priest assists as official witness representing Church and State, performs the prayers and ceremonies, and blesses the newlyweds in the Sacrament which they have conferred upon each other.

From ancient times Christian families have paid special attention to the religious preparation for marriage. It used to be the custom that engaged persons, if at all possible, would be given private rooms of their own, so they could spend some of their free time in prayer and meditation without being disturbed. There is also the excellent institution of Cana Conferences, or Marriage Preparation courses, founded with the idea that priests and experienced laymen could instruct engaged couples in the duties, problems and ideals of Catholic married life. Another even more important means of preparation is the making of a retreat before receiving the Sacrament of Matrimony.

Among the wedding presents in past centuries there was never missing an appropriate crucifix for the new home, a religious picture or statue for the family shrine and a few religious books (including a family Bible) to start the domestic library of the newlyweds.

A famous custom from medieval days is the so-called "St. Joseph's Night." Newly married people perform some devotions together on the night of their wedding, asking God's special blessing upon their married life. Then they spend the night in peaceful rest, observing voluntary abstinence in honor of St. Joseph, the patron of Christian families. It is a significant fact that modern doctors suggest this very same practice of abstinence during the night of the Wedding Day for medical and psychological reasons.

When the newlyweds are settled in their home after the honeymoon, it is an ancient custom to invite a priest to come and bless the house or apartment. The *Roman Ritual* provides a liturgical form of this "Blessing of Homes." We give here the main prayer in English translation:

> Bless, O Lord, almighty God, this home, that therein be found good health, chastity, the power of spiritual victory, humility, goodness and meekness, the plenitude of the Law, and thanksgiving to God, the Father, Son and Holy Spirit; and may this blessing remain on the home and on its inhabitants now and forever. Amen.

Like other human conditions and attitudes, happiness in marriage depends to a great extent on training and self-training from early youth. In our time, when children see and hear so much about "love," they should know that most of the things which the world calls love have nothing at all to do with the true and great virtue of love; that true love does not consist in, or aim at, selfish pleasures, but seeks devoted service and sacrifice for the genuine good of those whom we love; that marriage, and what leads up to it, must be based on the virtue of true love, so pleasing to God and blessed by Him.

One of the most impressive and practical customs I have ever encountered is this little prayer, which some parents of my acquaintance have taught their children to say every night from their fourteenth birthday on: "Dear Lord, show me what is Your holy Will. If You want me to serve You as a priest or religious, help me with Your light and grace. If it is Your holy Will that I should marry, please send me the one whom You know to be best for me and who will build up with me a happy and holy family, as You want it to be." It is not difficult to see what effect such a prayer must have in the life of a boy or girl who says it every night from his or her early teens.

It is a widespread vogue today that even the younger teen-agers must have "friends" of the other sex. To prevent such friendships altogether will not be possible, because the children are surrounded by them wherever they go and are expected to practice the custom as a matter of fact. Conscientious parents will carefully supervise the company of their children without, however, exasperating them. One of the best methods is to have the youngsters bring their friends home and enjoy their parties right in or around the house. Thus, the parents will always know with whom the children keep company.

Some parents, especially mothers, are tragically thoughtless and conceited about this point, as if their own children were free from the effects of Original Sin, from inordinate inclinations, sensuality and temptations. So-called modern "fashions" captivate them, with the result that they see no danger or wrong in immodest dress, in dangerous company, in sensual amusements and in the complete freedom of their daughters to go out alone with boyfriends by day or night.

Some time ago a story was published in a Catholic magazine of how a 15-year-old girl in a Catholic summer camp sneaked out one night and spent the whole night with a boy from the neighborhood on the shore or in a canoe on the lake. Next morning, when this was found out, the priest who served as chaplain of the camp was quite upset. He called the mother of the girl on the phone, told her shortly what had happened and asked her to impress upon the child at her next visit how dangerous and wrong this was.

"I am shocked, Father," answered the lady, "and I shiver

at the thought of what might have happened. At my visit this weekend I shall certainly talk to her and make it clear to her that this must never happen again. If she goes out like this again, she must take a sturdy boat and not a fragile canoe, which could overturn so easily."

PRIESTHOOD

"A new priest's blessing is worth a pair of shoes." This ancient proverb is inspired by the high esteem our ancestors had for the holy priesthood. What it means is this: The blessing of a newly ordained priest is so precious that, in order to receive it, a person should willingly walk even so far as to wear out a pair of shoes on the road. This appreciation of the "first blessing" of a priest is still fresh and keenly alive in most of our modern Catholic families, and children are deeply impressed by it, especially if the purpose and power of a priest's holy calling is explained to them.

However, the blessing of a priest should not only be sought in the first days after his ordination, but later on as well, whenever the occasion arises. Hence, the age-old custom in Catholic families that parents try to have some priest drop in for a short visit once in a while. Before he leaves, they ask for his blessing, which is received by the whole family kneeling devoutly in front of him. This custom is also helpful in teaching the children respect for the priesthood, coming, as they do, in personal contact with the priest at an early age. They experience something of what the children in the Holy Land must have felt when Our Lord in His loving-kindness took them into His arms, talked with them and blessed them.

On the first possible occasion, older children should be taken by their parents to an ordination. We have appropriate booklets which explain all the details and meanings of the beautiful and impressive ordination rite. Thus, our youngsters will gain a deep and lasting appreciation of the priesthood, its various duties and powers, its great holiness and dignity.

Attentive participation in these ceremonies might achieve more than words could do in planting the seed of a priestly vocation in the hearts of boys.

Here again our ancestors had the right instinct and "feeling with the Church." It was a general practice to keep ordination day as a public holyday in European cities during the past centuries so everyone could attend the solemn rites in the cathedral. Similar customs prevail even today for the first solemn High Mass of a new priest. In the Catholic sections of Europe, the entire town celebrates the first High Mass of one of its sons. All buildings are festively decorated, the young priest is conducted in solemn procession from the house of his parents to the church, and the whole day is kept as a feast day by all inhabitants.

It was the general custom among Catholics to greet priests on the street and in public in order to profess the Faith and show reverence for the holy priesthood. When I was a little boy, my mother told me, "You must always joyfully greet a priest, whether you know him or not. Your Guardian Angel, too, greets the priests with great love and reverence." These simple words of my mother made a deep impression on me; I never forgot them. May God inspire our Catholic parents to keep this wonderful custom alive in our time, to honor God in His priests and to bear witness to our union with the Church.

Finally, there is the practice of common family prayer for priests and for new vocations to the priesthood. These "priest-prayers" (usually the Rosary) are said by the family on Ember Days because the Church has officially designated those days for such prayer, according to Our Lord's word, "The harvest indeed is great, but the labourers are few. Pray ye therefore the Lord of the harvest, that he send forth labourers into his harvest." (*Matt.* 9:37-38). Lately the laudable custom has spread of devoting a Saturday every month (Priest-Saturday) to the reception of Holy Communion and prayer for the priests, asking God through Mary's intercession that He bless and sanctify our priests and grant the Church many holy vocations.

3

FAMILY PRAYER

Going home from church, the newlyweds are not going out of the spiritual atmosphere into a worldly one. They are not leaving the Sacrament behind in the house of God. Their union in marriage, their home and their hearts must remain filled with the grace and love of the Lord. A family is actually a little kingdom of God.

These thoughts have prompted Christians at all times to express their union with God, not only as individuals, but also as a family. It was the ancient custom among Catholics that, at least once a day, father, mother and children would gather in the home for common prayer. This practice deeply impresses its lasting mark on the hearts of the children. It is not only an addition of individual praying, but a special source of grace and blessings which far transcends the power of an individual's prayer and unites us with the Lord more deeply and intimately, according to His own word, "Where there are two or three gathered together in my name, there am I in the midst of them."

If this is true of any group, how much more does it apply to the prayerful union of parents and children! In fact, it is a common experience that even the small children who cannot yet talk, quickly adjust themselves to the spirit of devotion when the whole family prays. They seem to be inspired by the grace of Baptism, which gives them an instinctive grasp of the supernatural far beyond their natural capacities. Held in the arms of the mother, such a little child will watch the praying family with large and solemn eyes, even try to fold his hands and assume an attitude of reverence, which is entirely different from his usual behavior.

When parents sometimes complain that their smaller children are not quiet or silent in church, perhaps the reason is in many cases that their children have never breathed the atmosphere of prayer at home. There is a radiance of warmth and attractive dignity about a father and mother who not only give their children the example of individual prayer, but join with them in a common practice of devotion and family prayer.

In recent times this practice has died out in many homes. Some people still keep a trace of it in the form of grace at meals; but even this custom is fast disappearing, especially among the younger ones. They are either ashamed or careless, or they persuade themselves there is not enough time to pray before meals. Thus many a "Catholic" home never unites the family in common prayer, to the great spiritual loss of each individual member.

Thank God, in recent years the practice of the family Rosary has spread far and wide. Besides obtaining graces and blessings, it has also resulted in a revival of family prayer. All those who have at heart the kingdom of God in the home can do no better apostolic work than spreading the family Rosary among their friends.

Even in our attendance at liturgical services, especially Holy Mass and Communion, the participation of the family as a whole should be the ideal. It is a pity that practical considerations make it seem necessary in many churches to separate the children from their parents on Sunday, that special children's Masses should have to be held at which the parents are not allowed, and vice versa. Our Lord loves every good family so much that one cannot help thinking how greatly He would enjoy seeing parents and children together at His Holy Sacrifice and receiving Him together, as a family.

Besides the act of prayer, there are many ancient customs of sanctifying the home through the use of the sacramentals of the Church: holy water, blessed candles, food blessed by the priest on certain feast days, blessed palms,

Easter water, etc. We shall speak of these sacramentals at various points in the following chapters.

As we have the altars and shrines in our churches, so a Catholic family would do well to keep a simple but dignified shrine in the home. It would be a symbol to all members that their lives belong to God, that religion and prayer are not merely a Sunday affair, and that the home of Christians is a holy place. How cold are the houses and homes in which no trace of a religious object is found!

Parents are well advised not to overload the family shrine with all kinds of statues and pictures and pious equipment. Such tasteless exaggerations either cause a certain resentment in the hearts of children or lead them along the path of unwholesome sentimentality. The same may be said about many products of religious "art" which are nothing but cheap and repulsive pieces of sloppy mass manufacture. The way many statues and pictures represent the Blessed Virgin, for instance, is a shameful aberration. Mary never looked like these images of modern beauty queens, with sensual features; nor was she made up with paint, lipstick and rouge, as some statues and pictures show her. A sense of true appreciation for what is wholesome, solid and really beautiful in religious art is shockingly lacking in many families.

More and more Catholic homes in the United States are adopting the custom of Mary gardens. A fairly large statue of the Blessed Virgin is placed outside the house, surrounded by nature's tribute of trees, shrubs and flowers. This is not only an honor to Our Lady and a public profession of our faith, but also a powerful encouragement of our devotion to Mary and a source of pious inspiration for many who behold this beautiful sight.

4

HOLY WATER

According to the *Roman Ritual,* holy water is blessed by the priest and mixed with blessed salt. Water is a symbol of cleansing and wholesomeness, salt a symbol of purity and freshness. Among the many sacramentals of the Church, holy water is one of the most ancient and most universal. Although produced in a liturgical ceremony and used at liturgical services, it is also intended by the Church to be reverently used by the faithful in their homes. The *Ritual* even has a special notation to this effect:

> The faithful may receive holy water in their own containers and take it home to sprinkle it on their sick ones, their houses, fields, vineyards and other objects; also, they may keep it in their homes to sprinkle themselves with it every day, and even often during the day.

Actually, the earliest use of holy water in the Latin Church was intended exclusively for the homes of the Christians. At that time it was not blessed in church, but in the houses of the faithful by priests. Only in the seventh century did they begin to bless it in church and use it for liturgical purposes. People sprinkled it on themselves as a protection against the attacks of evil spirits and as a help in sickness and disease. These two purposes are still mentioned in the official prayer of blessing:

> . . . that in the service of Thy holy mysteries this water may become powerful through divine

grace to drive out the demons and to avert sickness. May whatever is sprinkled with it in the homes of the faithful be freed from all impurity and harm. Let neither the breath of pestilence nor the air of corruption (contagion) take hold there. Let all the wiles of the hidden enemy be dispelled, so that whatever should threaten the well-being or the peace of the inhabitants may vanish through the sprinkling of this water. Grant us that the blessing of welfare which we implore through the invocation of Thy holy Name may be defended from all hostile aggression. Through Christ our Lord. Amen.

According to the ancient custom in all Christian countries, a holy water font is affixed near the door-frame of a room and the faithful cross themselves [make the Sign of the Cross] coming and going, with a pious invocation of God's loving mercy. Thus the use of this sacramental becomes a means of frequently lifting your mind and heart to God in the midst of your day's busy life.

It is certainly in keeping with the spirit and intention of the Church if you will revive this ancient custom of having a holy water font in your home. Teach your children to use this sacramental with understanding and piety. What a consolation if, at the time of sickness, you sprinkle it with a prayer on your suffering dear ones!

On Sundays and on the eve of great feasts it is customary in many places that parents sprinkle holy water through the home, to sanctify it and to symbolize the fact that each Catholic home should be a little kingdom of God.

Finally, why not bless your children with holy water every night or "even often during the day" as the *Ritual* says? Worldly people might smile about such a practice and consider it a queer relic of old-fashioned piety. The eye of faith, however, clearly beholds the radiant light of grace and the spiritual fruit which this simple but deeply religious act will produce in the hearts and lives of your children.

−5−

THE SIGN OF THE CROSS

Like holy water, the Sign of the Cross is intended by the Church not only for liturgical usage, but also for frequent use by the faithful in private devotion and in their homes. It is a symbol and prayer in one unit, professing both our faith in the Holy Trinity (words) and in our redemption by Christ (gesture). Already in earliest times the Sign of the Cross symbolized the renewal of Baptism.

In the earliest Christian centuries the faithful made the Sign of the Cross with three fingers on their foreheads. St. Augustine (431) mentions and describes it many times in his sermons and letters. So did most of the ancient Fathers and writers of the Church. Long before Augustine, in the third century, Tertullian had already reported this custom of early Christian practice: "In all our undertakings—when we enter a place or leave it; before we dress; before we bathe; when we take our meals; when we light the lamps in the evening; before we retire at night; when we sit down to read; before each new task—*we trace the Sign of the Cross on our foreheads.*"*

Is it not a pity that so many of our Protestant friends, who sincerely claim to follow the practices of early Christianity, have abandoned the custom of making the "Sign of

---

*Tertullianus, *De Corona*, Chap. 3; *Patrologia Latina*, vol. 11, col. 80. Publisher's note (1998): Of course, the Sign of the Cross is now usually made by tracing a cross with the right hand touching the forehead, breast, left shoulder, right shoulder, then joining the hands.

Christ"? Even greater is the pity that many Catholic families have discontinued making the Sign of the Cross on those traditional occasions mentioned by Tertullian. Years ago it still was a general practice that children crossed themselves devoutly before starting their homework or going into the water to swim; families would make the Sign of the Cross before and after meals (accompanied by a short prayer), and all would cross themselves with holy water when leaving or entering the home.

Children should be taught very early to make this holy sign with reverence and devotion and to pronounce the sacred words correctly. Some time ago I visited a young Catholic family. The mother proudly showed me the "first thing" she had taught her two-year-old child. It was a dance step accompanied by a few words of singing and a rhythmic waving of arms. The little girl performed with obvious enthusiasm and a good deal of self-consciousness.

Later, before leaving the house, I asked the mother: "Does Katie know how to make the Sign of the Cross?" "Why, no," said she, "Katie is much too young for that." How thoughtless some parents are!

THE BLESSING OF CHILDREN

In her motherly love and care, the Church provides a number of liturgical ceremonies for the blessing of children. They are to be performed by the priest according to the *Ritual*. One, for an individual child, may be used either at home or in church. The other one is more solemn, to be used for blessing a group of children in the church. Then there is a special blessing of babies; a blessing of expectant mothers; and a special blessing of mothers after giving birth, which includes a blessing of their babies (this is the so-called "churching"). Another touching formula of blessing is provided for sick children.

All these blessings are yours for the asking. Why do you parents not avail yourselves of the great opportunity of having your children blessed by the priest? Someday when a priest is about to visit your home, especially on a holyday or some other festive occasion, ask him beforehand to bring along his *Ritual*. Have some holy water ready, and let him give this wonderful blessing of the Church to your dear children.

Besides these official blessings, there is the ancient custom of a simple and private blessing which the parents themselves give their children by making the Sign of the Cross on their foreheads. While doing this, they usually say, "God bless you and protect you," or, "God bless and keep you," or, "God bless you and bring you back safe and sound," or some similar phrase, as the occasion requires.

This Catholic custom was universal in all countries before the Reformation. It is still practiced in Catholic sections of Europe and America. In Ireland the mother makes the Sign of the Cross on the children's foreheads when they leave the house to go to school or church. In France and French Canada, the father blesses his whole family, mother and children, on New Year's Day. In Central Europe, too, this custom is still widely kept. In my own family, our mother blessed us children every night in this manner. It is one of my first memories how she made the Sign of the Cross on our foreheads and wished us a good night. This simple action taught me more than any words the great truth that parents are God's representatives.

When the children are grown, the parents' blessing will not be given so frequently. But on leaving for extended trips, on special occasions like entering religious life or on their Wedding Day, it may still be conferred upon them. Many a Catholic man may be seen in European or Canadian railroad stations bowing his head and receiving his mother's blessing before boarding the train.

The Bible often speaks of the great and powerful effect of a parent's blessing. Perhaps there would be less trouble with our modern youngsters, less vandalism and juvenile delinquency, if more of our parents would bless their children every day from babyhood on. In fact, a Catholic mother could well start with this custom from the day her child is born.

This blessing of children by their parents is one of the precious items of our Catholic inheritance. These days there is a special good reason for it, besides the ones already mentioned. We live at a time when radio, television, comics, movies and human company compete in filling the minds of your children with worldly thoughts and imaginations. A mother's blessing every night will go far in counteracting dangerous influences on the children's hearts and souls.

BAPTISMAL NAMES

In our day, when even Christian parents often choose their children's names without regard to hallowed traditions, the Church still strongly insists that a Saint's name be give in Baptism, at least as the middle name, whenever the chosen first name is not of Christian origin or significance. It is an ancient tradition that children be given the name of a Saint whom later they should come to know, to love and to venerate.

It is sad to behold how many parents overlook the importance and great meaning of this religious tradition. Of all things a person can acquire in this life, his name is the first and closest possession; in a way, it is himself. When Our Lord was to be born, God did not leave the choice of the name to human beings. He Himself chose the Saviour's name and considered it important enough to send an Angel to announce His choice to St. Joseph.

Today a child's name is given in a similar supernatural setting. When the sacred liturgical ceremonies of Baptism come to their peak, at the very moment the Sacrament is performed, the priest solemnly announces the name of the child. As the light of a heavenly beacon, originating together with baptismal grace, this name accompanies you through life. If you are a woman and marry, your last name will be changed—but your baptismal name remains forever, a beautiful symbol of the Sacrament's lasting mark on your soul.

No wonder that Christians have always considered it a matter of great importance to give their children names which would have a special religious meaning and significance, the names of God's favorite friends. Fortunately, many of our modern first names are abbreviations or alternate forms of Saints' names, although the parents do not realize it. They should try to find out what the name means that they would like to give their child. If it does not in any way represent a Saint's name, then they might be well advised to consider another choice, or at least connect it with a Christian name (like Shirley Ann). In fact, if the parents neglect the choice of a Christian name, the Church directs the priest to add one of his own choice in Baptism.

Our children should be instructed from their earliest years about the meaning of their names. Mother can explain to them who the Saint was whose name they bear. They should be taught to pray to him every night, to love him and to consider him a special heavenly friend and protector.

The great advantage of this familiarity with the personal Patron Saint lies in the fact that children thus acquire a lasting, deep and solid spiritual relation to Saints. There is no danger of mere emotionalism or sentimentality, as often happens later if they make their first acquaintance with Saints in the Catholic school. This early relation to the Patron Saint is based on the bedrock of objective realities, not on mere sweet feelings. For what is more real to a child than his own self, identified by his own name? And if this name presents to the little one the figure, life and story of a great Saint of God, it is easy to see what influence it will exert on him.

THE NAME-DAY

The celebration of birthdays is not the original practice in Catholic homes. It only spread within the past few centuries, replacing the earlier Christian custom of observing the feast day of the Saint whose name was acquired in Baptism.

The celebration of Saints' feasts is a part of the liturgical life of the Church. Thus any person observing the feast of "his" Saint immediately enters into the warm sphere of liturgical radiation and spiritual enrichment. Compared to this, the celebration of the birthday is more worldly, merely natural and almost accidental in its lack of significance.

It is not necessary that we do away with our customary birthday celebrations. But we should certainly try to restore the meaningful Catholic tradition of celebrating the feast of the Saint whose name was given in Baptism and who is our personal patron, loving and helping us whether we observe or neglect his veneration. Children will surely not object to the keeping of the "name-day," for to them it will mean, besides all its other significance, another personal feast day every year.

If a child has been taught to pray to his Patron Saint every night, he will greet the feast of this Saint with a thrill of joy and spiritual elevation. It is his "own" feast, and the whole family should make him happily aware of it. After all, birth is a common event shared with the same significance by all members of the family. The Patron Saint, however, is not usually shared with brothers or sisters, thus making his feast so unique and exclusive, at least in its psychological aspect.

According to ancient traditions, the name-day is festively held in Christian homes. I remember how from early childhood I went to church with my father every year on the feast of St. Francis Xavier, attending the Holy Sacrifice and later receiving Communion, too. Returning home, I found the table cheerfully decorated with flowers and little presents. Mother, Father, brothers and sisters offered their congratulations. Then we sat down to a joyful breakfast, my proud little self sitting in the place of honor. And all this because centuries ago a wonderful young man in Spain loved God so much that he became a Saint. I cannot express the powerful conviction that filled me every year on this occasion, *how great and important it is to become holy.* This was one of the eloquent lessons which our religious customs taught me without words, but with an effect greater than many words could achieve. Judging from this aspect, we may truly say that such Catholic customs in the home educate the children more efficiently than the best Catholic teachers could ever do in school.

As a parish priest I have often asked children about the Saints whose names they bore. It is tragically sad to see how few of them in our time have any idea who their Patron Saint was. They know nothing about him, they do not know when his feast is kept, they have no devotion to him. These same children, however, know most of the Hollywood stars and television celebrities; they (at least the boys) know the make of every car at a quick look; they know the names and achievements of the players on football and baseball teams. Only the Saint whose name is theirs they do not know.

Who is to blame for this ignorance? There is only one answer: the parents. Do not say, "The nuns should explain these things in school." That would be too late. It has to be done when the children are three or four years old. And who can teach them at that age but Mother and Father?

What has been said above we adult people might as well apply to ourselves. Do you know your Patron Saint? Do you celebrate his feast with Mass, Holy Communion and special prayer? Do you daily invoke his loving help and protection? You can achieve a great task of the apostolate that might spread its influence down to future generations if you will restore in your family the Catholic custom of venerating the personal Patron Saints and of celebrating the name-days.

THE CELEBRATION OF FEASTS

In the liturgy of the Church, every day of the year is a "feast" observed with the greatest and most solemn act of celebration at our disposal: the Holy Sacrifice of the Mass. The feast days of Our Lord, of the Blessed Virgin and other Saints revolve in a glorious annual cycle of supernatural light, just as the sun, the moon and the stars do in the natural order.

In the Catholic family these daily feasts can be celebrated too, at least by a spiritual union with the Holy Sacrifice. The greater feasts of Christ and Mary and some feasts of Saints are connected with traditional observances in the home. Most of this pious inheritance has been lost in recent times. But a goodly number of seasonal customs have survived, even in our modern day, like the Christmas and Easter customs. Their original religious meaning, however, is no longer known to most people. It is the religious meaning of these observances which will be described and explained in the following chapters.

Besides the common and main celebrations of the year, each family might wish—for one reason or another—to observe particular feasts of Christ, Mary or the Saints as a sort of private family affair. The more we have of such joyful celebrations in our homes the better. Many families still preserve the knowledge of how, according to national background, such days were kept with charming traditions in the "old country." Why not renew this precious folklore? Many of its details could easily be adapted to modern conditions.

Happy the children who grow up in a home that is rich in traditional celebrations! Their lives will be more full and radiant through the inspiration of this childhood experience. Faith, culture, emotional security, absorbing joy, satisfaction of mind and heart, a warm spirit of love and union in the family, sound development of character and personality traits, appreciation of true values: these are some of the fruits which a childhood of such joyful family celebrations produces.

Christian fathers and mothers in our time cannot dispense with careful planning and supervision of their children's activities and amusements. How precious, then, are the helps and means which wholesome tradition provides! Every family should have some of the books that give explanations, suggestions, sketches, texts and programs for happy celebrations in Catholic homes.

To assist the parents in this effort, we print here a short list of recent books and pamphlets in which they will find ample material for the understanding, planning and execution of such family feasts for many days of the year:

Maria Augusta Trapp, *Around the Year with the Trapp Family,* 251 pp., Pantheon, New York.

Mary Reed Newland, *The Year and Our Children,* 328 pp., P. J. Kenedy & Sons, New York.

Francis X. Weiser, S.J., *The Christmas Book,* 188 pp., Harcourt, Brace & Co., New York.

—Same author, *The Easter Book,* 224 pp., Harcourt, Brace & Co., New York.

—Same author, *The Holyday Book,* 220 pp., Harcourt, Brace & Co., New York.

K. Burton and H. Ripperger, *Feast Day Cookbook,* 194 pp., McKay Co., New York.

Edgar Schmiedeler, O. S. B., *Your Home a Church in Miniature* (3 pamphlets), Washington D.C.

Helen McLoughlin, *Family Advent Customs* (pamphlet), Liturgical Press, Collegeville, Minnesota.

—Same author, *Christmas to Candlemas in a Catholic Home* (pamphlet), Liturgical Press, Collegeville, Minnesota.

—Same author, *Easter to Pentecost Family Customs* (pamphlet), Liturgical Press, Collegeville, Minnesota.

Therese Mueller, *Family Life in Christ* (pamphlet), Liturgical Press, Collegeville, Minnesota.

Elsa Chaney, *The Twelve Days of Christmas Book*, Liturgical Press, Collegeville, Minnesota.

Florence L. Berger, *Cooking for Christ,* National Catholic Rural Life Conference, Des Moines, Iowa.

Publisher's note (1998): Most of the above-listed titles are out of print, but can perhaps be obtained through used book dealers or libraries (especially through interlibrary loan).

—Part Two—

SEASONAL CUSTOMS

−10−

ADVENT

The holy season of Advent is a time of spiritual preparation for the "Coming" of the Lord. It is a threefold Coming of Christ for which we should prepare our souls. First, the celebration of His coming in the past, two thousand years ago, when He was born at Bethlehem, just as we celebrate our own birthday every year. Then His Coming in the present, in Mass and Communion and with many special graces, on Christmas Day. Finally, His Coming in the future, when Heaven will start for us and when we shall greet Him in the bliss of eternal glory, if only we die in His grace.

Children have a keen understanding of these various aspects of preparation in Advent. Some parents, however, do not seem to be interested enough in meditating on and understanding these truths themselves, and so are not able to explain them to their little ones. Thus, the joyous anticipation of the feast is restricted in many homes to the very features that are least important, especially since their original religious meaning is no longer understood, like the figure of Santa Claus, the Christmas tree, the presents, the Christmas displays in department stores, the symbols and festive decorations in the home. All this amounts to a shallow spirit of joy and excitement.

True preparation for Christmas must be centered around the liturgical thoughts mentioned above and manifested by daily prayer. All members of the family should be acutely aware that love of Christ, prayer, personal holiness and some penance are the main features of the Advent season. External customs and symbols should never disturb, but only deepen, this spiritual attitude.

It is not the multitude of practices that guarantees greater spiritual fruit, but perseverance and intensity. Explain to your children the message of the Advent wreath, then light the candles every day and have your family say some prayers in front of it, and you will achieve a better religious preparation for Christmas than by using six or seven different customs and practices all at once. There are many ways of doing such things in the home. They all are good and useful—but it is better to concentrate on one or two of them which seem to fit best into your particular circumstances.

In the following chapters, various means and customs will be described of celebrating the holy seasons of Advent and Christmas with spiritual fruit. There should be enough individual details in these traditions to provide you with the inspiration needed for your own family and with ample material for making an appropriate selection.

One negative demand has to be stressed in our time if you truly wish your family to observe Advent in the spirit of holy liturgy. Modern commercialism has introduced the abuse of starting the Christmas celebration on Thanksgiving Day, of displaying the Christmas symbols through all the weeks of Advent, and of presenting Christmas music on radio and television a whole month in advance of the feast. The spirit of Advent, a spirit of prayerful penance and meditation, is utterly absent from these displays. Such untimely anticipation of the Christmas festivities tends to rob the feast itself of a joyful and radiant celebration. No wonder a 13-year-old boy was heard to remark: "By the time Christmas comes I am sick and tired of it."

Christmas does not start until the evening of December 24 [or, strictly speaking, until December 25 begins at midnight]. After the dark and dawn of Advent it should rise like a glorious sun before the eyes and hearts of our children, sudden and fresh in all its joyous features.

What can we do about it? Since it is not possible to stop the abuses which commercialism has introduced (unless enough parents protest), you can only try to protect your family from this harmful influence. As far as possible, do not let your children listen to Christmas music and Christmas programs in Advent. Do not take them to see the displays in department stores except perhaps during the last few days before the feast. Do not allow them to go to Christmas parties long before December 25. (This abuse is sometimes practiced even in Catholic schools and organizations.) Do not decorate your home before Christmas Eve.

Instead, try to explain to your children why they should co-operate willingly in avoiding all such premature celebration of Christmas. After all, we do not sing "alleluia" on Good Friday either, nor do we hold an Easter parade on Holy Thursday.

THE ADVENT WREATH

This charming symbol connected with the season of Advent has not only found its way into America, but has of late been spreading so rapidly that it is already a cherished custom in many homes. People seem to welcome it with eager delight wherever they are introduced to this "new" custom. Actually, it is centuries old, although not as old as most other Christmas traditions.

The Advent wreath originated a few hundred years ago among the Lutheran population in Eastern Germany. It seems to have been suggested by one of the many light symbols which were used in folklore at the end of November and beginning of December. At that season of the year our pre-Christian forefathers began to celebrate the month of Yule (December) with the burning of lights and fires. The Christians in medieval times kept many of these light and fire symbols alive as popular traditions of ancient folklore.

In the sixteenth century, somebody conceived the fortunate inspiration of using such lights as a religious symbol of Advent in the houses of the faithful. This practice quickly spread among the Protestants of Eastern Germany and was soon accepted by Protestants and Catholics in other parts of the country.

The Advent wreath is exactly what the word implies, a wreath of evergreens (yew or fir or laurel), made in various sizes. It is either suspended from the ceiling or placed on a table, usually in front of the family shrine.

Fastened to the wreath are four candles [three purple, one pink] standing upright, at equal distances. These candles represent the four weeks of Advent.

Daily at a certain time (usually in the evening), the family gathers for a short exercise of prayer. Every Sunday of Advent one more candle is lit until all four candles shed their cheerful light to announce the approaching birthday of the Lord. Before the prayer starts, all other lights are extinguished in the room and only the gentle glow of the live candles illuminates the darkness.

The Advent wreath has no direct connection with the liturgy of the Church. It is not a sacramental, the *Ritual* contains no special blessing for it, and the Church has never officially proclaimed its symbolism.

Catholic families may have the wreath blessed with a general blessing given by the priest if they so wish *(Benedictio ad omnia)*. A special liturgical blessing could be given to the candles, since the Church provides such a blessing *(Benedictio candelarum)*.

The traditional symbolism of the Advent wreath reminds the faithful of the Old Testament, when humanity was "sitting in darkness and in the shadow of death" *(Luke* 1:79); when the Prophets, illumined by God, announced the Redeemer; and when the hearts of good people stood in flame with the desire for the Messias. The wreath itself symbolizes the "fulfillment of time" in the coming of Christ and the glory of His birth. (The wreath is an ancient symbol of victory and glory.)

After some prayers, which are recited for the grace of a good and holy preparation for Christmas, the family sings one of the traditional Advent hymns or a song in honor of Mary. In some sections of Europe, it is customary that persons with the name of "John" or "Joan" have the first right to light the candles on the Advent wreath and the Christmas tree, because John the Evangelist starts his Gospel by calling Christ the "Light of the world," and John the Baptist was the first one to see the light of Divinity shining about the Lord at His baptism in the Jordan.

It is hard to picture the wonderful memories which such a daily custom in Advent evokes in the hearts of those who enjoyed its inspiration in their childhood. Somehow these holy moments of prayer and prayerful song before the lights of the Advent wreath exert an influence in later life which seems out of proportion with the simple ceremony.* Actually, it is not, of course; for to this practice of family prayer with its beautiful symbolism apply the words of Christ: "For where there are two or three gathered together in my name, there am I in the midst of them." (*Matt.* 18:20). You had Christ in your home when you were a child. This is the brilliant truth that makes such a simple tradition so meaningful.

---

*It is now customary for the candles to be lit thus: first week (one purple candle)—by youngest child; second week (the first purple candle plus another purple candle)—by oldest child; third week (first two purple candles plus the pink candle)—by the mother; fourth week (all four candles)—by the father. The Advent wreath prayer for the week is the Collect or Prayer from the Sunday's Mass. This can simply be followed by the grace before the evening meal. See Appendix 2.—*Publisher*, 1998.

–12–

ST. NICHOLAS

One of the most beloved Saints all through the Middle Ages was St. Nicholas of Myra. In fact, he still is the favorite Saint of little children in the Catholic sections of Europe. This veneration is easily explained: He was, and still is, a special Patron Saint of small children. His feast day, December 6, is a great day of celebration for the little ones.

In many parts of Europe children still receive his "visit" on the eve of his feast. Impersonated by a man wearing a long white beard, dressed in the vestments of a bishop, with mitre and crozier, he appears in the homes as a heavenly messenger. Coming at the start of Advent, he admonishes the children to prepare their hearts for a blessed and holy Christmas. He examines them on their prayers. After exhorting them to be good, he distributes fruit and candy and departs with a kindly farewell, leaving the little ones filled with holy awe.

I still vividly remember the annual visit of this friendly and saintly figure on the evening of December 5. With joy and happy excitement we awaited his coming. We were convinced, as little children easily are, that he really was our great Patron Saint who came from Heaven on his feast day to visit us children whom he loved so much.

With utter sincerity we promised him to overcome our faults, to obey our parents and to prepare our hearts for Christmas. Gratefully we accepted his gifts and kissed the ring on his holy hand. Never again in all my life have I experienced the unspeakable thrill of a physical nearness to

Heaven as I did on those evenings of my childhood when "St. Nicholas" came to us. When I later found out that it was not really the Saint but a man representing him, this caused me no shock or harm. The thrill I had felt remained in my memory and has remained to this day with all its beauty.

This, then, is the true and original form of the "visit of St. Nicholas." The date is the evening of December 5. The whole purpose and meaning of this custom is deeply religious, educational and of wholesome emotional value.

We do not advocate that this practice of the "visit" of St. Nicholas be restored.* What we advocate very much, however, is a revival of the veneration and annual celebration of the Saint, who is still patron of little children. (The Church has never "deposed" him from this spiritual patronage.) Our Catholic parents would do well to pray to St. Nicholas themselves, that his intercession may help them in the training of their little ones.

Explain to your children that they have a special Patron Saint in Heaven. Tell them his legend (see pages 43-45). Teach them to love him and to pray to him every day. Make them look forward with joy and anticipation to the feast of their Patron Saint.

On December 6, allow your little ones a happy celebration in honor of St. Nicholas. Congratulate them, give them small presents, arrange some special enjoyments, have a "festive" meal (which can be very easily prepared for children). And do not forget some prayers to the Saint. Mother could pronounce the words and have the children repeat them. Included in this prayer should always be the petition that St. Nicholas may help them to prepare their hearts for a very good and holy Christmas.

In Europe they have thousands of small figures of the

---

*Some families have revived an alternate form of celebrating St. Nicholas Day: The children set out their shoes on the evening of December 5; the next morning, they find that their shoes have been filled by "St. Nicholas" with sweets and small presents.—*Publisher*, 1998.

Saint, dressed as bishop, for sale every year before December 6. Perhaps Catholic mothers in this country might find a way to make or provide such a figure for their home. It would certainly delight our little ones to have an image of their Patron Saint, not a picture or statue, but a figure with a "real" white beard and with "real" bishop's clothes. (Dad might help with his hobby tools.)

LIFE AND LEGEND OF ST. NICHOLAS

Very few historical facts are known about the Saint. He was Bishop of Myra in Asia Minor. Emperor Diocletian cast him into exile and prison during the persecution at the beginning of the fourth century. Released by Constantine the Great, he returned to his city. There he died about 350. Italian merchants brought his body from Myra to Bari in Italy (in 1807), where his relics are still preserved. The reports of numerous miracles ascribed to the Saint before and after death are based on a long tradition.

By the year 1200, St. Nicholas had captured the hearts of all European nations. Many churches, towns, provinces and countries venerate him as their Patron Saint. Merchants, bankers, seamen and prisoners made him their patron, too. But his main patronage is the one over little children. All these patronages are derived from details of his inspiring legend, which might be told to the children as follows:

St. Nicholas was born of a rich family in the city of Parara in Asia Minor. When he was very little, he lost his mother and father by death and had to lead a lonely life as an orphan. After he had grown to young manhood he decided to devote his life entirely to the service of God and to good works for his fellow men. Obeying the words of Christ, he distributed all his possessions to the poor, the sick and the suffering. Quite often he helped poor children by putting gifts of money through their windows during the night, when nobody could see him.

His love for Christ inspired him to make a pilgrimage to

the Holy Land and to visit the places where Our Lord had lived and died for us. On this trip a terrible storm arose, but Nicholas miraculously saved the already sinking ship by his prayers to God. That is the reason he is now venerated as their Patron Saint by many brave sailors all over the world.

When he returned from this pilgrimage, the bishops of Asia Minor selected him as successor to the bishop of Myra, who had just died. The whole town rejoiced when they heard this good news. Nicholas received the Holy Orders modestly and devoutly. As bishop he led a very holy life. He prayed and fasted to convert sinners with the grace of God; he preached to the people and instructed the children in the Faith. He also practiced a boundless love for his fellow men by great kindness and charity. Having been an orphan himself, he now became the beloved father of orphans. After teaching the children, he would often delight them with many little gifts.

Under the Roman Emperor Diocletian, who persecuted the Christians, St. Nicholas was arrested, taken away from his home by the pagan soldiers and thrown into a prison. He suffered the hardships of hunger, thirst, loneliness and chains. He wanted to die as a martyr of Christ. But when Emperor Diocletian left his throne and the first Christian Emperor, Constantine the Great, ruled the Roman lands, all Christians who were suffering in prison because of their faith were released. Among them was St. Nicholas. He returned to Myra, where he lived for many more years, a kind father to all his dear people, especially to the poor and the children.

One day he became very ill and soon realized it was time for him to go to Heaven. When he died, his soul was met by Angels, who conducted him to the throne of God with great joy and glory. The whole city mourned his passing, most of all the little children. But they knew that the Saint still loved them from Heaven, and so they began to pray to him. Their prayers were answered by thousands of favors, small ones and great ones. In this way the good Saint showed us that he did not forget the children and that he still loves them and helps them, if only they ask him. That is why little boys and girls everywhere now pray to their beloved St. Nicholas.

(The above "legend of St. Nicholas" was taken by the Author from his *Christmas Book,* with permission of the Publishers, Harcourt Brace & Co., New York.)

13

PREPARATION FOR CHRISTMAS

Besides the use of the Advent wreath, a number of traditions exist which are designed to help the Christian family, especially the children, in their preparation for the feast of Our Lord's Nativity.

Among public practices of this kind is the custom of holding a novena before December 25. In the Latin countries of Europe and South America, this novena is held as an evening devotion in church, with prayers and benediction of the Blessed Sacrament (*Novena del Niño*). In Central Europe it is a novena of Masses which are said early in the morning.

In the spirit of this ancient tradition, families could add a small feature to their daily Advent prayers to bring out the character of the novena. One suggestion might be to use the famous "O Antiphons," which in themselves form a kind of liturgical novena within the Divine Office. A good English translation may be found in the pamphlet, *Family Advent Customs,* by Helen McLoughlin (page 23 ff).*

For grown-up members of the family and for older children there could be no better way, of course, to make this novena than daily attendance at Mass, if possible.

Another custom, which originated in France but spread to many other countries, is the practice of having the little children prepare a soft bedding in the manger by using wisps of hay or straw as tokens of prayers and good works. Every

---

*The "O Antiphons" or "Greater Antiphons" are also found in the traditional *St. Andrew Daily Missal* following the Third Sunday of Advent. See Appendix 3 of this book (p. 109). —*Publisher*, 1998.

night a child is allowed to put into the crib one token for each act of virtue or devotion performed in preparation for Christmas. Thus, the figure of the Christ Child will find on Christmas day an ample supply of tender straw to soften the hardness of the manger's boards.

An old Catholic custom is the writing of "Christmas letters" by the small children. These letters, addressed to the Child Jesus (*not* to Santa Claus), are written or dictated by the little ones sometime before Christmas. They contain their wishes concerning presents, petitions for various intentions and a promise of sincere effort to please Our Lord in preparation for Christmas. When they go to bed, the children put their letters on the windowsill, from where "angels" take them during the night to bring them to the Child Jesus in Heaven. This charming custom helps the parents to impress on the minds of their little ones the importance of a sincere spiritual preparation and at the same time acquaints them with their children's desires and wishes for particular presents. Parents who favor this custom will often be deeply touched when they discover that some of their children put more stress on spiritual graces than on material gifts, even on an occasion like this.

Finally comes Christmas Eve, the day of immediate preparation. An atmosphere of joy and solemnity pervades the house. It is on this day (and not before) that the Christmas tree and all other decorations should be put up. The hearts of the children are filled with the spirit of the day, which alternates between devotion and happy excitement.

With a little effort on the part of parents, the activities of Christmas Eve could be organized into an inspiring unit of prayer, work and celebration. A division of tasks and a spirit of teamwork will heighten the joys of the day. According to ancient traditions, the evening meal might be arranged as a festive occasion. For the last time, the Advent devotion is held, and a little prayer or song might be included which expresses the thought of the glorious vigil, like this ancient prayer-hymn, inspired by the Introit of the *Rorate* Mass:

"Dews of Heaven, bring the Just One,
Clouds may rain Him from above!"
Thus the nations, still in darkness,
Cried for mercy, peace and love.
"Open, earth, and grow the flower
Radiant with grace and power!"
Lift your hearts, the time is near:
Christ the Lord will soon appear.

God the Son, in human nature
Was made flesh and dwelled on earth;
Life and light, in grace abundant,
He bestowed of priceless worth.
Men rejoice, exult with gladness;
Do not fear, dispel your sadness.
Raise your hearts, the time is near:
Christ the Lord will soon appear.

14

SANTA CLAUS

Many people think that Santa Claus is St. Nicholas "in disguise." Actually, the two figures have nothing in common except the name. When the Dutch came to America and established the colony of New Amsterdam, their children enjoyed the traditional "visit of St. Nicholas" on December 5, for the Dutch had kept this ancient Catholic custom even after the Reformation. Later, when England founded the colony of New York in the same territory, the kindly figure of Sinter Klaas (pronounced like Santa Claus) soon aroused the desire among the English children of having such a heavenly visitor come to their own homes, too.

The English settlers were glad and willing to comply with the anxious wish of their children. However, the figure of a Catholic Saint and bishop was not acceptable in their eyes, especially since many of them were Presbyterians, to whom a "bishop" was repugnant. Also, they did not celebrate the feasts of Saints according to the ancient Catholic calendar.

The dilemma was solved by transferring the visit of the mysterious man whom the Dutch called Santa Claus from December 5 to Christmas, and by introducing a radical change in the figure itself. It was not merely a "disguise," but the ancient Saint was completely replaced by an entirely different character. Some clever mind invented this substitution in the eighteenth century.

Behind the name Santa Claus no longer stands the traditional figure of St. Nicholas, but the pagan Germanic god Thor (after whom Thursday is named). To show the origin of the modern Santa Claus tale, let us give some details about the god Thor from ancient Germanic mythology:

Thor was the god of the peasants and the common people. He was represented as an elderly man, jovial and friendly, of heavy build, with a long white beard. His element was fire, his color red. The rumble and roar of thunder were said to be caused by the rolling of his chariot, for he alone among the gods never rode on horseback, but drove in a chariot drawn by two white goats (called Cracker and Gnasher). He was fighting the giants of ice and snow, and thus became the Yule-god. He was said to live in the "Northland," where he had his palace among the icebergs. By our pagan forefathers he was considered as the cheerful and friendly god, never harming humans, but rather helping and protecting them. The fireplace in every home was especially sacred to him, and he was said to come down through the chimney into his element, the fire. (See H. A. Guerber, *Myths of Northern Lands,* Vol. I, p. 61ff., New York, 1895.)

Here, then, is the true origin of our "Santa Claus." It certainly was a stroke of genius that produced such a charming and attractive figure for our children from the withered pages of pagan mythology. With the Christian Saint, however, whose name he still bears, this Santa Claus has really nothing to do. To be honest and historically correct, we would rather have to call him "Father Thor," or some such name.

Perhaps this will make it clear to parents why it is so difficult to explain "Santa Claus" as St. Nicholas. There is no basis for such an explanation; the two figures are entirely different. Considering the historical background, it might even seem better not to tell the children at all that "Santa Claus" is another name of St. Nicholas. Should we not rather let them consider St. Nicholas their Patron Saint (December 6) and Santa Claus, the delivery man of presents (December 24), as two completely unrelated figures, as they really are?

The fairytale of Santa Claus will not be abolished easily, despite the efforts of well-meaning people. Nor does it seem necessary. Children do like fairytales, and Santa Claus is one of the most charming of them. Catholic parents might use it without harm, provided they apply some safeguards to avoid an undue overstressing of the Santa Claus figure. Perhaps the following suggestions might help:

Keep the Santa tale in its simple, appealing form and shun the corruptions introduced by commercial managers, like Santason, Mrs. Santa Claus and similar repulsive features.

Never allow the figure of Santa Claus to dominate the child's mind. The Child Jesus must be the main figure in all his Christmas thinking. Picture to him Santa as merely a servant and deliveryman, delightful but not very important. I know a mother who had explained this to her children. One day she pointed out to them how Santa Claus was to be seen in every department store and how he drew so much attention to himself. The children found it highly amusing that this delivery-servant of God should try to make himself the center of the celebration. "He is a little dumb, isn't he?" said the girl, "but Jesus likes him and we like him, too."

Do not let your children present their wishes to Santa. If you want them to write down what they desire, let them write to the Child Jesus, according to the old Catholic custom. Santa does not give the presents; he only delivers what the Lord sends.

The above suggestions will also help to lessen the "shock" when the children find out that "there is no Santa." As one mother did when her little boy came full of doubts and asked her if there really was a Santa Claus, such a question should always be answered in truth—no matter how small the child is.

"Of course not," said the mother quietly, "that's only a story for very small children. You are a big boy now, so you understand how it really is. Our dear Lord does not need a delivery-man. He has already given you somebody who loves you very much and who is happy to give you the Christmas presents in His Name. Do you know who these persons are?"

The child thought for a moment, then he said, "Daddy and Mother?"

"Yes, my dear," answered she, "and would you not rather that Father and I give you the presents? We love you more than Santa Claus does."

"Why didn't you tell me that before?"

"Because it is nice for little children to believe in Santa. Aren't you glad you did?"

Again the boy thought for a minute. "Yes, it was nice," he said finally. Then he added, "But it's much nicer now."

Not every case can be handled exactly this way, of course. There are various ways of doing it. However, by following the general idea, parents will have no trouble in setting their children straight about the Santa tale when the right moment comes. The descriptions of great disappointment and psychological conflicts we often read about apply only to families where the parents have misled their own children by allowing Santa to take the central place instead of Christ, whose birthday is the only reason for the whole feast.

15

THE CHRISTMAS CRIB

The Christ Child in the manger and other pictures of the story of Bethlehem have been used in church services from the first centuries. But the crib in its present form and its use outside the church originated with St. Francis of Assisi. Through his famous celebration at Greccio (Italy) on Christmas Eve, 1223, with a Bethlehem scene including live animals, he made the crib popular. Since then it has been a familiar sight in Christian homes all over the world.

The crib should be a cherished part of the Christmas celebration in every family. It is not only completely religious in significance, but also presents to the children in a beautiful way the central event which we commemorate on this great feast. Thus it assumes the character of a religious shrine in the houses of the faithful during Christmas season. It should be placed in an honored position, on a table or some other support, not too high for the children to see it easily. Dignified decorations might enhance its attraction and solemnity.

It was, and still is, a custom in Catholic sections to "unveil" the crib on Christmas Eve in a ceremony of spiritual significance. Parents and children gather before the crib, and one of the older children reads the Gospel of Bethlehem. Then prayers are said and a Christmas carol is sung. At the conclusion of this simple rite, the members of the family wish each other a blessed and merry Christmas. It is at this moment that Christmas really starts in the home. Everything that went before was only preparation. This is the beginning of the feast, and its high points will be Mass and Communion a few hours later.

A crib for the family should be procured with care and loving effort. The setting could easily be created at the hobby bench during the evenings of Advent, Father and children helping together and using their imagination concerning the various details of structure, style and shape. The figures of the Holy Family, of shepherds and magi and animals, may best be bought in a store. Once acquired, they can be used for many successive years.

As the wreath during Advent season, so the crib may serve as a shrine for family prayer during the days of Christmas. The story of how St. Francis of Assisi "invented" the crib is so delightful and inspiring that it might be told or read to the children every year. We give here the account in the very words of Brother Thomas de Celano, who was there when it happened and who wrote it down:

> Blessed Francis called a friend about two weeks before Christmas and said to him: 'If you desire that we should celebrate this year's Christmas together at Greccio, go quickly and prepare what I tell you; for I want to enact the memory of the Infant who was born at Bethlehem, and how He was deprived of all the comforts babies enjoy; how He was bedded in a manger on hay, between an ass and an ox. For once I want to see all this with my own eyes.' When the good and faithful man had heard this, he departed quickly and prepared in the above-mentioned place everything that the Saint had told him.
>
> The joyful day approached. The brethren (Franciscans) were called from many communities. The men and women of the neighborhood, as best they could, prepared candles and torches to brighten the night. Finally the Saint of God arrived, found everything prepared, saw it and rejoiced. The crib was made ready, hay was brought, the ox and ass were led to the spot . . .

Greccio became a new Bethlehem. The night was radiant with joy. The crowds drew near and rejoiced in the novelty of the celebration. Their voices resounded from the woods, and the rocky cliff echoed the jubilant outburst. As they sang in the praise of God, the whole night rang with exultation. The Saint of God stood before the crib, overcome with devotion and wondrous joy. A solemn Mass was sung at the crib.

The Saint dressed in deacon's vestments, for a deacon he was (out of humility, St. Francis never became a priest, remaining a deacon all his life). He sang the gospel. Then he preached a delightful sermon to the people who stood around him, speaking about the nativity of the poor King and the humble town of Bethlehem.*

---

*(Quotation from Thomas De Celano was taken by the Author from his *Christmas Book*, with permission of the Publishers.)

16

THE CHRISTMAS TREE

Many writers derive its origin from the ancient Yule tree or from other light and fire customs of pre-Christian times. These explanations, however, are based on mere guessing and do not agree with the historical facts. It is true, people used to put up evergreen trees in their homes at Yule time; they still have Yule trees in Central Europe, side by side with the Christmas tree. But in order to explain the Christmas tree, we have to account for every traditional detail and show when, how and why it was introduced.

Surprising as it may seem, the use of Christmas trees is quite recent in all countries outside of Germany, and even in Germany it was not widespread till the beginning of the 19th century. The Christmas tree is completely Christian in origin, and modern historians have never been able to connect it with any particular custom of pre-Christian times. In fact, the whole idea and symbolism of the tree is entirely religious and based on the radiation of liturgical thought into Christian homes. It is a combination of two religious symbols from medieval days, the Paradise tree and the Christmas light. Here is the account of its origin.

From the eleventh century on, religious plays used to be performed in churches or in the open in front of churches. One of the most popular of these "mystery plays," as they were called, was the Paradise play. It represented the creation of man, the sin of Adam and Eve, and their expulsion from Paradise. This play closed with a consoling promise of the coming Saviour and of His Incarnation. For this reason the Paradise play was a favorite pageant in Advent.

The Garden of Eden was indicated by a fir tree hung with apples, from which Eve broke the fruit and gave it to Adam to eat. This "Paradise tree" attracted the attention of all onlookers, especially the children, since it was the only object on the stage.

During the fifteenth century the mystery plays were gradually forbidden by the bishops in all countries because abuses had crept in, like irreverence in acting, clowning of certain parts, non-religious additions, etc. The people, however, did not want to miss the Paradise tree. Since they could no longer see it in church, they started putting it up in their homes once a year, in honor of Adam and Eve on their feast day, which was December 24. The Latin Church has never officially celebrated Adam and Eve as Saints, but Eastern Churches do so, and from the East the custom of keeping their feast came into Europe. Thus, on December 24 one could see the Paradise tree in the homes of the faithful in various sections of Europe.

The very same day, however, is also Christmas Eve. A beautiful custom was practiced from early times on this day in all Christian countries, namely the "Christmas light," a symbol for Our Lord, the Light of the world that started shining at Bethlehem. This Christmas candle had been inspired by the liturgical usage of a burning candle to represent Christ. (We still have this symbolism in the Easter candle.)

In Germany, the Christmas candle used to be placed on top of a wooden structure made in the form of a pyramid, adorned with glass balls and tinsel. It was called the "Christmas pyramid." Now during the sixteenth century, people in Western Germany started to combine these two symbols which they had in their homes on December 24. Was not the Paradise tree a beautiful and live pyramid? Why not transfer the candles and decorations from the lifeless wooden pyramid to the tree?

This is exactly what they did. They took the lights, glass balls and tinsel from the wooden pyramid and put them on the Paradise tree (which already bore the apples). Thus our modern Christmas tree came into being. To indicate to their children that the Paradise tree was no longer a "tree of sin," but that it now symbolized the "light of Christ," the faithful suspended cookies and sweets beside the apples, to represent the sweet fruit of the Saviour's Redemption.

The Christmas crib which had been standing at the foot of the pyramid was now put under the tree. And the "star of Bethlehem" that had adorned the top of the pyramid was now fastened on the top of the tree. Thus, every particular feature of the Christmas tree is clearly explained as it actually developed through the combination of the two symbols, as modern research has shown.

Even today, in sections of Southern Germany, fir trees and branches decorated with apples, tinsel and lights are still called "Paradise." Another trace left by this origin is the fact that up to our time the fruits on the tree had to be round, representing the fruit of Paradise. Nobody would have thought of suspending bananas or grapes from a Christmas tree.

The first description of a Christmas tree with all its familiar features is given in a German manuscript of the year 1605. It was in the sections at the left bank of the Rhine that the tree developed, and from there it spread through the rest of the country, slowly at first, but with sudden great speed from about 1800 on. It came to America through the German immigrants towards the middle of the 19th century.

Considering these historical facts, it will be clear to parents how the meaning and message of the Christmas tree is completely religious. It stands in the house at Christmas time as a symbol and reminder that Our Lord is the "Tree of Life" and the "Light of the world." Its many individual lights might be explained to the children as symbols of His divine and human traits and virtues. The glittering decorations indicate His great glory. The fact that it is evergreen is an ancient symbol of eternity.

In keeping with this religious symbolism, the decorations of the Christmas tree should be appropriate and traditional. Silly figures of modern manufacture which disturb the dignified aspect of the tree should not be used. Sensational features like swirling glass candles, imitations of snow, Walt Disney animals, etc., do not fit its purpose and meaning. In radiant beauty and quiet solemnity it should proclaim in our homes the very message of the holy liturgy which has inspired its origin: *Lumen Christi*—"The Light of Christ."

17

OTHER CHRISTMAS CUSTOMS

LIGHTS IN THE WINDOWS

This custom was brought to America by the Irish immigrants. Its historical meaning and background are deeply inspiring and might be told to the children to make them understand the spiritual message which it contains. Smaller children usually forget such explanations from one year to the next and will have to be told again when the next Christmas comes. (From the Author's *Christmas Book*, with permission of the Publishers.)

When religion was suppressed in Ireland during the English persecution [17th century], the people had no churches. Priests hid in forests and caves and secretly visited the farms and homes to say Mass there during the night. Now it was the dearest wish of every Irish family in those days that at least once in their lifetimes a priest would be near their home at Christmas, so he could come and celebrate the divine Sacrifice during the Holy Night. For this grace they hoped and prayed all through the year.

When Christmas came, they left their doors unlocked and put burning candles in the windows so that any priest who happened to be in the neighborhood would know that he was expected and welcomed. The light of the candles guided him to the house. Silently he would enter through the unlatched door, to be received by the grateful people with tears of happiness. Their home was to be a church during the Holy Night.

The English soldiers, being suspicious of such customs,

asked the Irish what the purpose of this illumination was. In order to cover the actual reason, the Irish people used to explain: "We burn the candles and keep the doors unlocked, that Mary and Joseph, looking for a place to stay, will find their way to our home and be welcomed with open hearts." The English authorities, finding this Irish "superstition" harmless, did not bother to suppress it.

Thus the candles in the windows have always remained a cherished custom of the Irish, although many of them have forgotten its true reason and origin. From the Irish immigrants in this country, the custom spread among other Americans, and in many houses may now be seen the cheerful lights at Christmas time, radiating their message and greeting into the streets of the town.

We could and should tell the children this story of the lights in the windows and make them aware of the spiritual meaning of this attractive custom. Historically speaking, every such light is a herald of love and devotion to the newborn Saviour, of a burning desire for Mass and Communion on Christmas day and of heroic loyalty to the Church and the priesthood.

CHRISTMAS PLANTS

Our homes are decorated at Christmas time with traditional plants. Each one of these plants has its own story of how it came to be a Christmas plant and of its spiritual symbolism.

The "magic" plant of the mistletoe, called "All-heal" by the pagan Druids, was used in Christian times as a symbol of Christ, the Divine Healer of all nations.

The holly was a symbolic plant already with the early Christians. Its prickly points and the red berries resembling drops of blood reminded them that the Divine Child was born to wear a crown of thorns.

The clinging ivy is a picture of weakness upheld by strength from without. Thus it becomes a Christmas symbol in the home; we have to cling to our divine Lord in order to be holy.

Laurel (Bay) is an ancient token of triumph and glory. The Roman emperors used it for their wreaths of victory. As a Christmas decoration it aptly proclaims the victory over sin and death which the Baby of Bethlehem brought us.

From ancient times evergreens have been symbolic of eternity and everlasting life. This fact might be pointed out to the children at Christmas time. It will remind them that Our Lord is divine and eternal and that we are destined to share His everlasting life in the bliss of Heaven.

The poinsettia, a native plant of Central America, is now widely used in churches and homes, because its flaming color symbolizes the divine love of the newborn Redeemer. It also resembles the star of Bethlehem through the star-like arrangement of its red bracts.

Greeting Cards

In the middle of the last century people, began to send written greetings and good wishes to their relatives and friends before Christmas. It is claimed that the first Christmas card was engraved in 1842 by a 16-year-old artist in London. In America, the printing of Christmas cards was introduced by the Boston lithographer Louis Prang, a native of Breslau, Germany. Like all other products of his art, these first Christmas cards of Louis Prang are still famous among collectors because of their exquisite design and craftsmanship.

In 1890, however, a flood of cheap and gaudy "novelties" in Christmas cards was thrown on the market by manufacturers who were interested only in their own profits. Since then, abundant reason for disgust and disappointment with many of our Christmas cards has remained. Of the two billion cards mailed annually in America before Christmas, a great number do not show any appropriate designs, do not convey any message that would express or honor the central fact of the feast. Yes, there is a trend of late to return to the genuine spirit of the season. But too many Christian families and individuals are still indifferent; they thoughtlessly use Christmas cards which have nothing to do with the true meaning of the feast, or are of cheap, gaudy, sloppy and undignified design.

A wide field opens here for Catholic parents. By careful choice of your Christmas cards, you can impress upon your children the greatness of the feast and the importance of showing the true spirit of Christmas in all your actions. Also, an early training in the appreciation of true art and of its elevating beauty might be given to your children if you discuss and make the choice of your Christmas cards with them.

18

FROM CHRISTMAS TO EPIPHANY

The twelve days from the Nativity of the Lord to the feast of the Epiphany (January 6) were kept as a festive time from the early Middle Ages. Although this season is dominated by the observance of Christmas, it also has its own feasts and customs, which blend into the frame of the main celebration.

Almost every day a new element of devotion and joy is added to the treasury of family traditions. Fortunate indeed is the home that keeps these customs alive, where parents and children know how to honor and observe Christmas for twelve days, as the Church does.

DAILY DEVOTIONS

As already mentioned, a short Christmas devotion could be held on each of these twelve nights before the crib in the home. After January first, the figures of the Magi might be put up some distance from the crib and then moved nearer every day, to indicate their gradual approach to Bethlehem. Children draw great delight and inspiration from such symbolic gestures.

In some families this group of the Magi, with their servants and camels, "travels" through three or four rooms in order to reach the crib on the feast of the Epiphany.

ST. STEPHEN'S DAY

On the feast of St. Stephen, the first martyr of Christianity (December 26), the story of his life and death might be told to the children in simple words to explain the meaning of martyrdom. (See *Acts,* Chapters 6 & 7.) The crib could be decorated with red flowers. St. Stephen is also a protector of horses, and on this day farmers in Catholic countries bring their horses to have them blessed by the priest in front of the church. This might give the parents an occasion to explain the liturgical blessing of animals. We quote here the prayer of blessing for domestic animals from the *Roman Ritual.* It clearly shows what the Church intends and what she prays for when she blesses these animals:

O Lord, God, King of Heaven and earth, eternal Word of the Father, through Whom all things were created and destined for our support, look mercifully upon our humble prayers. As You have given Your assistance in our labors and needs, so deign to bless these domestic animals with Your heavenly blessing; through Your kindness and mercy protect and preserve them; and together with this earthly help, grant us, Your servants, Your eternal grace, that Your holy Name may be praised and glorified by our gratitude; Who livest and reignest with God the Father, in the unity of the Holy Spirit, God, forever and ever. Amen.

St. John's Day

Today (December 27) parents might explain to children the life of this holy Evangelist, who stood under the Cross when Jesus died. The Church bestows a special blessing upon wine today. It is an old sacramental in honor of the Evangelist, who, according to legend, drank a glass of poisoned wine without suffering harm because he had blessed it before he drank. Perhaps you can bring a bottle of wine to the rectory and ask the priest to bless it for your family? (The formula of blessing is in the *Roman Ritual.*) I remember how joyfully proud and excited I was on this day, since in our family all children of school age received a small glass of the blessed St. John's wine with our main meal. It did not taste very good to us, but it was "holy," and so we took it with great devotion.

THE HOLY INNOCENTS

December 28, the feast of the Holy Innocents of Bethlehem, is a festive day for little children, according to ancient tradition. In Catholic families, December 28 should be the "feast of babies." The babies themselves cannot consciously celebrate it, of course; but the rest of the family can, with some appropriate observance like decorating the baby crib, having a party "for the baby," and/or blessing the baby with the Sign of the Cross; and everyone can pray to the Holy Innocents for their intercession, that God may bless the baby in body and soul.

ST. SYLVESTER DAY

The last day of the year, the feast of St. Sylvester, is a splendid occasion for family óbservance. It is a tradition of centuries to visit Our Lord in a church on the evening of December 31, to thank Him for all the graces and blessing bestowed upon the family during the past year, and of asking His continued protection and help. At the family devotion in the evening, "Holy God, We Praise Thy Name" is sung by all. In many Catholic homes, it is also the custom that children, before going to bed, thank the parents for all their love, care and goodness. In France and French Canada, the father blesses all members of the family on this evening, or on New Year's Day, with the Sign of the Cross.

NEW YEAR'S DAY

This day, the octave of the Nativity, should actually be a "second Christmas" in the family. All the radiant features and details of the Christmas celebration might be repeated. For this reason, it is advisable to keep the Christmas tree and the decorations up until after New Year's. In fact, they should be kept until the day after Epiphany. This can easily be done if a little pot or can of water is placed around the foot of the tree to prevent it from drying out. In France, the presents are given on this day. In other sections, a part of the gifts is withheld at Christmas and kept for a second joyful present-giving on New Year's Day. This custom deserves to be highly recommended. It provides for the children an additional experience of thrill and happiness. Also, it prevents their being oversaturated with presents on Christmas Day, which usually makes them tired and unresponsive.

EPIPHANY

This feast is one of the greatest in the Church, and really a holyday of obligation. It is only by special dispensation of the Holy See that we do not keep it as a prescribed holyday in the United States. It commemorates the visit of the Magi at Bethlehem, when Our Lord manifested Himself as Redeemer to these representatives of the Gentiles, using the miraculous star to call them. Thus it becomes the central feast of the Catholic missions, and parents could well explain to their children the apostolate of our missionaries in foreign lands.

Epiphany is the last day of the Christmas celebration in the home. On the previous night, the Magi have "arrived" at the crib, their figures being neatly arranged in front of the manger, where they will remain until January 7 (or longer if you wish). For the last time, the Christmas tree is lit and the family holds its evening devotion before the crib. Some special features of solemnity or celebration might accompany the evening meal, a kind of "farewell to Christmas."*

---

*The Christmas season—Christmastide—actually extends through January 13, which is the octave of the Epiphany, but it also includes Candlemas Day, or The Feast of the Purification, which occurs on February 2. (*St. Andrew Daily Missal,* pp. xviii and 123). *—Publisher,* 1998.

Even the taking down of the Christmas symbols and decorations on January 7 can be turned into a traditional observance. Children could help to dismantle the tree and the crib, to pack the figures and decorations and store them away for another year. The bare tree (cut into pieces) and the twigs of evergreens might be burned in the fireplace or as a bonfire in the open (with the necessary precautions) on the evening of January 7, while parents and children sing a last carol and thank God for all the graces and joys of Christmas time.

Families who observe the feasts with joyful home celebrations, based on the religious thoughts of the season, will certainly never have to complain that their youngsters find home life dull and uninteresting. The modern trend of seeking shallow amusements outside the home is due mostly to the ignorance and inability of parents who forgot (or never knew) how to guide the lives of their children in the spirit of Christian tradition, with all its happy customs inspired by the holy liturgy.

-19-

YOU ARE MY VALENTINE

St. Valentine, a priest and martyr, died during the persecution of Emperor Claudius II, in 270. The day of his death, which became his feast day, was February 14. From early Christian times, young men and women on this day declared their love for each other, or chose a "steady partner" for a certain period of time. Our greeting cards on February 14 are a modern form of this ancient practice.

The connection of St. Valentine with this tradition of youthful courtship and love is not explained by legends, like his writing a letter to the daughter of the prison master, or February 14's being the day of mating for the birds. Such legends are of later date and were only invented to give some reason for the already existing custom.

The historical basis of the custom is the ancient Roman youth festival on the eve of the Lupercalia (February 14). The young people of the Roman Empire celebrated the day by declaring their love for each other, proposing marriage or choosing a partner for the following year (which started on March 1 in the centuries before Christ). This youth festival on February 14, with its pledge of love, stood under the patronage of the goddess Juno Februata.

When the Empire accepted Christianity, the worship and patronage of pagan gods naturally ceased. But the feast of youth continued, and so did the traditional customs. In place of the pagan goddess, however, they took as patron the Christian Saint whose feast day it was. Thus St. Valentine became the heavenly patron of youths and young lovers. They placed their affection, love, courtship and engagement under his care and protection. Keeping the ancient practice of choosing partners, they designated this relation by the name of the Saint. In countries which once belonged to the Roman Empire, this tradition was preserved through the Middle Ages. In England it endured even longer, and from there it came to the United States.

The words, "You are my Valentine," originally meant: "I offer you my comradeship of affection and love for (a certain period of time), and I am willing to consider marriage, if this companionship proves satisfactory for both of us." In this country the traditional meaning has been expanded to include all persons for whom a special affection is felt. Thus, the children send their cards to anyone they "love," in the sense of liking him very much.

Does it seem unreasonable to suggest that friendship and dating between young people could still be under the special protection of St. Valentine, the heavenly patron of youths and young lovers? Perhaps this ancient tradition might prove to be very valuable and helpful if revived again in its full meaning. Parents could certainly draw consolation from the fact that their children are conscious of this heavenly guidance and protection in the years of courtship and early love.

I know a family where the mother has taught her children to say a prayer to St. Valentine every night, that he may protect them in their companionships, guide their feelings of love and affection, preserve them from all dangers and strengthen their good intentions.

Even with smaller children, who send Valentine cards to the persons they like very much, this custom should not remain a mere formality. Parents could easily explain that such a message of sincere affection demands more than the mailing of a card. At least on St. Valentine's Day, if not oftener, the children should thank God for the precious gift of loving and affectionate friends, imploring St. Valentine's intercession and blessing for each one of those to whom they have sent their cards.

–20–

CUSTOMS OF LENT

Lent is a period set aside by the Church for fasting, self-denial and prayer, in imitation of Our Lord's fasting forty days and forty nights, and in preparation for the feast of Easter. It comprises forty days, not including Sundays, from Ash Wednesday to the end of Holy Saturday. According to the spirit and intention of the holy liturgy, Christian families observe this time of grace with many religious customs. Some of them, which might be helpful and appropriate in our modern homes, will be treated in the following pages.

CARNIVAL

From the fourteenth century on, the days before Ash Wednesday turned into a time of general feasting and worldly celebration, of eating, drinking, dancing, mummery, etc. Wherever these amusements are traditionally held, they have been accompanied by many excesses and abuses. Catholic families who live in sections where Carnival* is publicly kept might grant their children some good-natured and harmless enjoyment in the home, because the youngsters will clamor for a share in the general rejoicing; and the home is the proper place to give it to them.

At the same time, however, it seems advisable to explain to the children that the spirit of those days, despite the

---

*In Germany, Carnival is known as *Fasching*; in the United States, as *Mardi Gras. —Publisher*, 1998.

worldly Carnival revelries, is one of penance, devotion and atonement. The Sunday Masses of pre-Lent [Septuagesima, Sexagesima and Quinquagesima Sundays] and the liturgical rules reflect this character. The *Gloria* is omitted in the Mass, purple vestments are worn by the priests, and a more severe tone characterizes the various official prayers.

In medieval times the faithful used to go to Confession on Tuesday before Ash Wednesday, in preparation for Lent. That is why we call it "Shrove Tuesday" (the day on which people are "shriven"—absolved—from sins).

In 1748 Pope Benedict XIV instituted a special devotion for the three days preceding Lent, in order to offer prayers and atonement for the many sins and scandals committed at Carnival time. This devotion, called "Forty Hours of Carnival," is still held in places where the carnival frolics are of general tradition. The Blessed Sacrament is exposed in the churches all day.

For Catholic families who live in such places, it is a custom that one or two members visit a church of exposition every day and spend some time in adoration, prayer and atonement before the Eucharistic Lord, who is being seriously offended by many people during those days.

Ash Wednesday

At the beginning of Lent the Church administers to her children the ancient sacramental of the imposition of ashes. These ashes are made by burning the blessed palms of the previous year. They are solemnly blessed by the priest, then imposed on the heads of the faithful in the form of a cross, with the words: "Remember, man, that thou art dust, and unto dust thou shalt return."

This ceremony is a symbol of penance and sorrow for our sins. In the early Christian centuries, it was only used for public sinners, but around the year 1000 the popes and all the faithful started to receive the ashes as a sincere and external token that we all are poor sinners.

These things might be explained to the children, so they will benefit from the understanding of the sacramental which they receive on Ash Wednesday. It should be a powerful reminder for them that they must start a time of special penance and cleansing of their hearts through prayer, contrition and self-denial.

On Ash Wednesday a family devotion might be held which expresses the spirit of the season. Also, some external sign of Lent might suitably be arranged in the home, like removing all flowers from the family shrine, or replacing the statue of Christ by a crucifix, or some other such gesture of symbolic significance.

FASTING AND PENANCE

The grown members of the family who are obliged to fast should on occasion explain the law of Lenten fasting and its practice to the children, so they will understand its purpose and meaning. Also, the term "penance" should be made clear to them. It does not mean sacrifice and self-denial in the first place, but a "change of heart," a victory over sin and a striving for holiness. The sacrifices of fasting and self-denial are only means and signs of this spiritual penance.

If children understand this well, they will not put the main effort in Lent on technical feats of abstaining from pleasures (which sometimes make them proud or vain), but in sincere contrition, prayer and humble fight against their faults. Only on this basis, and with this motivation, should they be encouraged to practice some little acts of self-denial like abstaining from certain delicacies (candy, chocolate) or pleasures (movies, comics, etc.).

It would seem a wholesome suggestion to make the children aware that it is a much better penance to do what is necessary than to abstain from what is not necessary. "Obedience is better than sacrifices." (*1 Kgs.* 15:22). What good are external acts of penance if a child, while abstaining from candy, stubbornly fights every day against Mother's order to do the dishes or to perform some other chores, and if he neglects his schoolwork or constantly harasses brothers and sisters with his unfriendly behavior?

LENTEN FOOD

A traditional means of reminding the family that it is the holy season of Lent is the Lenten foods, which are served only at this time of the year. Thus, parents and children realize, even at their meals, that prayer and penance should be practiced during these days.

Apart from meats, anything might do as "Lenten food," so long as it is not usually prepared in the same way during the rest of the year. In some countries it was customary to bake the buns with an indentation in the form of a cross (cross buns). In other places, certain soups are served only in Lent (bread soup, lentil soup, spinach soup, etc.). In many families, the desserts are made without sugar frosting or whipped cream during Lent. [Or, dessert may be entirely omitted from meals.] There are many ways of indicating the holy season by the choice of certain Lenten foods. Any one of them is good, as long as it is reasonable in itself and serves the purpose of reminding the family of Lent.

Perhaps the easiest, and at the same time the most significant, Lenten food custom for our time might be to serve a small pretzel to every member of the family with his main meal in Lent. It sounds surprising, but the pretzel has a deep spiritual meaning for Lent. In fact, it was the ancient Christian Lenten bread as far back as the fifth century. In the old Roman Empire, the faithful kept a very strict fast all through Lent: no milk, no butter, no cheese, no eggs, no cream and of course, no meat. So they made small breads of water, flour and salt. To remind themselves that Lent was a time of prayer, they shaped these breads in the form of arms crossed in prayer (in those days they crossed their arms over the breast while praying). Therefore they called the breads "little arms" (*bracellae*). From this Latin word the Germans later coined the term "pretzel."

Thus the pretzel is the most appropriate food symbol in Lent. It still shows the form of arms crossed in prayer, reminding us that Lent is a time of prayer. It consists only of water and flour, thus proclaiming Lent as a time of fasting. Besides, it is a custom come down to us from the early Christians, who had invented it as bearer of such a great spiritual message. (The earliest picture and description of a pretzel—from the fifth century—may be found in the manuscript-codex No. 3867, Vatican Library.)

That many people eat pretzels today all through the year, that they take them together with beer in taverns and restaurants, is only an accidental habit. The true purpose and meaning has been forgotten. However, the pretzel still is an image of arms crossed in prayer; it still is the symbol of prayerful penance in Lent. In many places of Europe pretzels are served only from Ash Wednesday to Easter, thus keeping the ancient symbolism alive.

There seems to be no reason why our Catholic families should not return to this beautiful custom of our ancient Roman fellow-Christians, especially since we still have these breads around everywhere. The children will be delighted and greatly impressed when they hear the true story of the pretzel. And such a pretzel at their dinner plate every day during Lent will certainly proclaim its spiritual message as clearly and deeply to them as it did to many a Christian in ancient Rome.

−21−

HOLY WEEK

Palm Sunday

The palms, which are solemnly blessed in the church and distributed by the priest on Palm Sunday, should be kept reverently in the home throughout the year. Usually they are attached to a crucifix or holy picture, or put to the left and right of the statue on the family shrine. They are a sacramental intended to bring blessing and protection upon those who use them, as the liturgical prayer of blessing proclaims:

> Bless, O Lord, we pray Thee, these branches of palm; grant that what we Thy people outwardly enact in Thy honor, we may inwardly fulfill with utmost devotion, by triumphing over the enemy and by attaching our hearts above all else to Thy merciful words of redemption.

On Ash Wednesday or Palm Sunday of the following year these palms might be burned, perhaps best in the back yard, and the ashes buried in the ground. This little ceremony will teach the children that objects which have become sacramentals through liturgical blessing are not to be thrown away like other things, but should be destroyed by nature's agents (fire, water, soil).

Spring Cleaning

According to an ancient tradition, the three days after

Palm Sunday are devoted in many places to a thorough cleaning of the house, the most vigorous of the whole year. Carpets, couches, arm chairs and mattresses are carried into the open and every speck of dust is beaten out of them. Mother and children scrub and wax floors and furniture, change curtains, wash windows and dispose of all superfluous or unusable articles that have accumulated in the course of months. The home is buzzing with activity.

No time is wasted on the usual kitchen work; the meals are very casual and light. On Wednesday night everything has to be back in place, glossy and shining.

This traditional spring cleaning, of course, is to make the home as neat as possible for the greatest feast of the year. It seems that the custom was taken over from the ancient Jewish practice, for the Jews in the Old Testament cleansed and swept and decorated the whole house in preparation for the feast of the Pasch (Passover).

It will be good for the children to co-operate in a part of this cleaning when they come home from school. It keeps them busy with a task that has a special meaning and significance not only for the external celebration of Easter, but also in a symbolic way, with their internal preparation for the great feast.

Besides, it occupies them with an activity different from their usual interests after school time, and thus it reminds them that Holy Week is different from all other weeks. Finally, if it means a burden and sacrifice to them, so much the better. By giving up their play and games and helping mother in the cleaning of the house, they do some very practical and wholesome penance in honor of the Lord's Passion.

THE SACRED TRIDUUM

The last three days of Holy Week have always been a time of special observance in Christian homes. They are a period of quiet, recollection and prayer. In many places, even today, people lay aside their usual occupations in order to have ample time for prayer, meditation and attendance at church services. Children stop all noisy games and amusements. No music instruments are played; radio and television are not used, except for appropriate religious programs; no comics are read, and all members of the family fast a little more than during the rest of Lent.

This atmosphere of penitential devotion and quiet during the three great days of Holy Week is an experience that deeply affects the children and helps them more than any words could do toward an understanding of how important Christ's Passion is for each one of us. It also induces them to meditate, mourn and pray with all sincerity. Thus, the grace of God is poured into their hearts and great supernatural blessings are given them in these days.

Parents and older children who attend the solemn services of the holy liturgy, as they were restored in their original form by Pope Pius XII, should not fail to procure and use some of the booklets recently published which explain the services and provide an English translation of the sacred texts. If at any time mere attendance is not sufficient but conscious participation in the sacred rites is called for, this certainly applies to the triduum of Holy Week.

HOLY THURSDAY

This is the traditional day for a very devout and fruitful Easter Communion. If at all possible, it should be received by the whole family together. Here the ideal is supported by a certain pressure of necessity, thank God. Since there is only one Mass on Holy Thursday in most parish churches, the members of a family going to Communion will have to receive at the same time. So, why not take one more step and go willingly, consciously, as a family unit of parents and children together?

In many homes, the memory of the Last Supper is brought out by the arrangement of the main meal in the evening. Of late the custom has been suggested in various books and pamphlets, of imitating the ancient Passover meal, even in its details: A yearling lamb is to be roasted and served with bitter herbs and a brown sauce; Jewish matzos, together with wine, are to be distributed by the father in silence to all members of the family, thus commemorating the institution of the Blessed Sacrament.

The use of some pious "ritual" at the supper on Holy Thursday is surely to be recommended. However, an imitation of the Last Supper of Our Lord in its details does not seem to be advisable. Children, with their gift of keen and faithful observation, might easily conceive the ritual at the family table as a "photographic" reproduction of the Last Supper and thus acquire inaccurate and unhistorical notions about it. To mention only one example, are we sure that Christ used *massah* (unleavened bread) of the shape and size of modern Jewish "matzos"?

Starting on Holy Thursday, a little family devotion might be held with those children who are too small to go to church for the services. On each of the three days the events commemorated could be explained to them and a few prayers said with them before the family shrine.

GOOD FRIDAY

Good Friday was always observed in the Church as a day of mourning, fasting and prayer. Since the Reformation, however, some sects have tried to bestow upon it a joyful note. This practice certainly does not represent the spirit of early Christianity. The *Apostolic Constitutions* (fourth century) call Good Friday a "day of mourning, not a day of festive joy," and St. Ambrose (c. 340-397), Archbishop of Milan, termed it a "day of bitterness on which we fast." (*Sancti Ambrosii Epistolae, Patrologia Latina*, vol. III, col. 12).

The note of sadness, mourning and prayer is expressed in all the solemn and beautiful rites of the Good Friday liturgy. Now that this liturgy has been restored to its ancient form, the faithful may also receive Holy Communion on this day.

It is an old custom among Catholic populations that on Good Friday parents and children are especially recollected and quiet all through the day. Even the meals are taken in silence in many homes. Children do not go out to play with their friends, but walk to church instead, to pray the Stations. There is no doubt that such pious observance places a certain strain on the youngsters. They are willing, however, to carry this burden if the parents prudently inspire and encourage them. Only children who sincerely and willingly perform some of these penances will taste the fullest measure of a glorious and overflowing Easter joy.

A very appropriate and helpful occupation for children on Good Friday would be the slow, meditative study of good reproductions of classical religious art, showing scenes from the life, the Passion and the death of Our Lord. It will not be too difficult for the average family to buy and collect such picture albums of the great masters. We have excellent and inexpensive editions of religious art reproductions. These could be kept in the home as visual education aids for parents and children, both for spiritual meditation and for the appreciation of good art.

HOLY SATURDAY

Since the anticipated vigil service on Holy Saturday morning was abolished by Pope Pius XII and its liturgical celebration again placed in the evening hours, or during the night, the spirit of the whole day has returned to its original significance. It commemorates Christ's rest in the tomb. No services are held in the churches all through the daylight hours. It is only at night that the Easter vigil starts, with its deeply impressive ceremonies. It is a night of prayer and joyful expectation, until finally the *Alleluia* proclaims the exultant message of the Resurrection and leads us to the glorious celebration of Easter in the Holy Sacrifice.

In the home, the spirit of Holy Saturday should still be one of devout recollection, but a note of relief and peace will replace the sadness of Good Friday. Parents and children could busy themselves with various preparations for the feast, refraining, however, from premature celebration. The family shrine might be rearranged and decorated with special solemnity for the Easter season.

We should like to appeal to Catholic parents that they allow their children of school age to attend the Easter vigil service in church. In many places this service is held in the evening of Holy Saturday and thus presents no great difficulty for the attendance of smaller children. Those who cannot easily follow the sacred rite by reading the booklets might have the meaning briefly explained by the parents.

22

EASTER SYMBOLS AND CUSTOMS

NEW CLOTHES

The tradition of wearing new dresses and apparel on Easter Sunday is practiced by many people in this country, even by those who otherwise pay little attention to the spiritual side of the feast. Strange as it may sound, this custom too goes back to the early centuries of Christianity. It has a deep religious meaning, which could and should be consciously restored in our modern observance.

The early Christians, who were mostly baptized during the solemn Easter vigil on the night of Holy Saturday, used to wear white gowns through the whole Easter week, as a symbol of the grace of Baptism, which had cleansed them from all sin and made them pure and holy before God. The other Christians who had already been baptized in previous years did not wear white garments, but they dressed in new clothes at Easter to indicate that they, too, had risen to a new life in Christ through penance and prayer during Lent. Thus the wearing of new things at Easter was an external profession and symbol of the Easter grace, of a spiritual resurrection to a better and holier life.

This custom has been kept in Christianity ever since and has come down to our day. Most people, however, have forgotten its spiritual meaning. In a Catholic family, Father or Mother should explain to their children what this tradition really means. When the youngsters go out on Easter Sunday all dressed in new things, they will then not suffer from feelings of empty vanity, but will happily wear their finery in honor of the Risen Christ, as a symbol of their love and loyalty and as a public profession of gratitude for the spiritual grace and blessing of the feast.

EASTER PARADE

Our modern Easter parades originated during the Middle Ages as a religious custom which is still kept in its ancient form in sections of Central Europe. Dressed in their best clothes, the people take the so-called "Easter walk" after the High Mass of the feast day. They march in a well-ordered column through the town and into the open countryside. A crucifix decorated with flowers—or in some sections the Easter candle—is borne at the head of the procession. At certain points on the route, they recite prayers and sing Easter hymns.

After the Reformation, this traditional Easter walk lost its religious character in some countries and was continued only as a popular custom. From England it came to America and developed here into the famous Easter parades held annually in our big cities on Easter Sunday.

Catholic families who take part in the Easter parade should be aware of its religious origin and meaning. Its purpose is to profess publicly that we believe in Christ's Resurrection and that we wish to announce and to bring Easter blessings and Easter joy from the altar of God into the whole world around us.

Children to whom this true purpose of the Easter parade has been explained will walk in it with a spirit of devotion and joyful profession of their loyalty to the Risen Saviour, and not with the vain desire of having their finery seen and admired.

EASTER LAMB

The Easter lamb, representing Christ, with the flag of victory, is the most significant symbol of the festive season. It may be seen in pictures and images in the homes of most families in the Catholic parts of Europe. The liturgical use of the Paschal lamb as a symbol for the Saviour inspired the faithful of medieval times to eat lamb meat on Easter Sunday. In fact, for centuries, the main feature of the popes' Easter dinner was roast lamb.

In modern times the custom developed of having an image of the Easter lamb made of pastry or sugar [or a lamb-shaped cake] as the centerpiece of the table during the Easter meal. This custom could easily be adopted by our Catholic families. It would provide a distinctive and appropriate symbol as main decoration at the festive meal and remind the children of the joyful feast.

Besides the image of the Easter lamb as the centerpiece on the table, ancient traditions call for a special and attractive decoration on Easter Sunday. In many countries the Easter table is adorned with flowers, ferns, candles and colored Easter eggs. After the prayer of grace before dinner, the words are added: "This is the day which the Lord has made, alleluia"; and the answer is given, "Let us be glad and rejoice, alleluia."

EASTER WATER

In the liturgy of Holy Saturday night the officiating priest solemnly makes the sacramental of Easter water, which the Church provides for the faithful to take home. It is to be used like holy water, to sprinkle on persons, house and rooms during the Easter season.

A very pertinent custom would be for Catholic families to sprinkle the food on the Easter table with it. This will mark the Easter dinner as an unusually solemn and festive occasion and confer upon it the special blessings which the Church wants all good things to have on the "feast of feasts."

EASTER EGGS

In ancient times, eggs were a symbol of spring and fertility. An egg seems dead and yet contains new life; so does the earth at the end of winter. This is the reason why people in pre-Christian ages presented each other with eggs at the beginning of spring (which in those days also was the beginning of a new year).

In medieval times the eating of eggs was prohibited during Lent. So the custom of giving eggs was transferred to Easter Sunday. Instead of representing fertility, the Easter egg now became a symbol of the rock tomb, out of which Our Lord gloriously emerged to the new life of His Resurrection.

This is a beautiful symbolism that will forever associate the Easter egg with Christ's Resurrection in the minds of children, provided it has been clearly explained to them. They will then also readily understand why the Church has given us in her *Ritual* a special blessing of eggs at Easter time. Here are the words of this blessing:

> We beseech Thee, O Lord, to bestow Thy benign blessing upon these eggs, to make them a wholesome food for Thy faithful, who gratefully partake of them in honor of the Resurrection of our Lord Jesus Christ.

In accordance with this religious aspect of Easter eggs and of their Christian symbolism, it might be suggested that children receive their first Easter eggs within a little ceremony at breakfast on Easter Sunday. The cheerful colors and designs of the eggs remind them of the joy they should have on the day of Christ's Resurrection. If the Easter eggs have not been taken to church for the official blessing, father or mother could sprinkle them with Easter water or holy water before the meal begins.

EASTER BUNNY

Hares and rabbits served our pre-Christian forefathers as symbols of fertility (because they multiply so fast). They were kept in the homes and given as presents at the beginning of spring. From this ancient custom developed the story of the "Easter bunny" in Germany, in the fifteenth century. Little children believe that Easter eggs are produced and brought by the Easter bunny. This is one of the traditional fairy tales which delight the small children. However, it has no deep meaning, nor any religious background.

In fact, the Easter bunny has never assumed a religious symbolism like the Easter egg. Neither in liturgy nor in folklore do we find these animals connected with the spiritual significance of the Easter season, and there is no special blessing for rabbits or hares in the *Roman Ritual*.

The only religious note concerning the Easter bunny is the explanation given in some countries to the children that white bunnies remind us, through the snowy color of their fur, how great the purity and innocence of our souls should be, not only at Easter but at all times.

EASTER PASTRY

In many sections of Europe people serve traditional breads and pastries at Easter, like the Russian Easter bread (*paska*), the German Easter loaves (*Osterstollen*), the Polish Easter cake (*Baba Wielkanocna*), etc. Very often these breads and pastries, together with meat and eggs, are blessed by the priest on Holy Saturday.

It might be suggested that some similar custom of serving special kinds of bread or pastry at Easter be introduced in our homes to enhance the appreciation of the great feast in the hearts and minds of the children. Such exclusive little features on festive occasions capture their imagination and teach them spiritual lessons in a gentle and natural manner.

EASTER HAM

The custom of eating ham at Easter derives from the pre-Christian symbolism of the pig. This animal has always been a token of good luck and prosperity among the Indo-

European nations. Even today we still have the custom of "piggy banks," which express the wish for good luck and prosperity to the saving youngsters.

Based on this symbolism, the eating of pork was a tradition for all solemn occasions. In Christian times this ancient practice was retained like the serving of the "boar's head" at Christmas in England, and the eating of ham in many countries at Easter. Our modern Easter ham, therefore, symbolizes the spirit of solemnity, joy and happiness which we should rightly have and show on the day of Our Lord's Resurrection.

The Church does not provide a particular blessing for Easter ham, but only for Easter lambs, Easter eggs, Easter breads and new fruits at Easter. The ham, however, can be included in the liturgical formula of blessing for food in general (*Benedictio Comestibilis Cuiuscumque*).

EASTER LILIES

The Easter lily is larger than the more generally known Madonna lily. It was introduced in Bermuda (from Japan) at the middle of the last century. In 1882 the florist W. K. Harris brought it to the United States and spread its use here. Since it flowers first around Easter time in this part of the world, it soon came to be called "Easter lily." The American public immediately accepted the implied suggestion and made it a symbolic feature of the Easter celebration. Churches began using it as a decoration on Easter day, and people adopted it as a favorite in their homes for the Easter solemnities.

Although the Easter lily did not directly originate from a religious symbolism, it has acquired that symbolism, and quite appropriately so. Its radiant whiteness, the delicate beauty of shape and form, its joyful and solemn aspect, certainly make it an eloquent herald of the Easter celebration. Besides, lilies have always been symbols of beauty, perfection and goodness. The Holy Scriptures, both of the Old and New Testaments, frequently make use of this symbolism.

Our Lord once showed the Apostles some lilies and said:

"Not even Solomon in all his glory was arrayed as one of these." (*Matt.* 6:29). Now, since Jesus Himself stated that lilies are more glorious than the greatest earthly splendor, is it not fitting that we use these beautiful flowers to glorify Him on the day of His Resurrection? Why not explain to the children this symbolism of the lily and then have some Easter lilies at the family shrine or on the dinner table during the festive season?

23

VENERATION AND FEASTS OF MARY

The Mother of God

From earliest childhood, the little ones in a truly Christian family are taught to know, to love and to venerate the Blessed Virgin. Her main privilege and her greatest title, that she is the Mother of God, should be explained first and foremost. All other titles and privileges of Mary can then be easily deduced and explained on the basis of this greatest one. Thus the children will from the very start have a clear and correct notion of Mary's outstanding dignity and holiness, and of the main reasons for it.

The Church herself, with the instinct that the Holy Spirit confers on her, has shown this in a practical way. In the second part of the Hail Mary, she chose among all titles of the Blessed Virgin only this central privilege as a part of this great invocation: "Holy Mary, *Mother of God*, pray for us sinners . . ."

Have your children understand very clearly that they cannot honor Mary more highly than by devoutly proclaiming her as the Mother of God. Thus they honor Christ at the same time and will, in their own small way, atone for the betrayal of Our Lord by so many modern "Christians," who consider Him a "great man," but deny His divinity.

Prayer to Mary

One of the first prayers taught children by their parents is the Hail Mary. Later on, when they will ask their questions about babies and birth, the words, "Blessed is the Fruit of thy womb," can fittingly serve the mother as the basis for a simple and reverent explanation that will satisfy the curiosity of her little child.

The common family prayer should always include at least a short invocation of the Blessed Virgin. If the family Rosary is said by parents and children together, special stress might be laid on a dignified manner of pronouncing the words. Though it is not necessary to think of these words while the Rosary is being recited (because the meditation on the Mysteries may occupy the mind), the devout performance of the prayer will help much towards internal devotion and spiritual warmth.

On feast days of Mary, and perhaps on Saturdays too, some special prayer to the Blessed Virgin might be added to the regular family devotion. If there is no common prayer, the parents should at least see to it that their children offer some additional prayers to the Blessed Virgin at their individual evening prayers.

It might be good to explain at an early date how powerful and important are the prayers which the Church, together with her faithful, addresses to Mary and St. Michael after every Low Mass. These prayers were prescribed by Pope Leo XIII to obtain God's special help and protection against all enemies of our holy Faith. Pope Pius XI directed the intention of these prayers primarily toward the conversion of Russia. Here, too, the children will be sincerely impressed by the great purpose of these prayers, if it is only explained to them. Later on in their lives they will keep this in mind and not rush out of the church before these important prayers are said.

THE SCAPULAR

When children are older, it has been a long-standing practice in many Catholic families to have them enrolled in the brown scapular of Our Lady.

With membership in the confraternity of the holy scapular, the child acquires a new and closer personal relation to the Blessed Virgin. It is a true dedication which involves the benefit of many graces and spiritual privileges, but also demands a greater measure of prayer and devotion. Parents should take care that their children, before being enrolled, do clearly understand the meaning, privileges and duties of their membership in the scapular of Our Lady and are sincerely determined to carry out their obligation.

The Sodality

This is another religious organization which creates a particular bond between the child and the Blessed Virgin. The purpose of the Sodality is not only to consecrate its members to Mary and inspire in them a special devotion to her, but also to train them, under the help and guidance of their heavenly Queen, in a life of determined self-sanctification and apostolate.

Catholic parents will consider it a great honor, and openly show this attitude, if one of their children has been found worthy to join the Sodality of Our Lady. The day of reception should be celebrated as a feast in the family, with special features of congratulation, solemnity and joy.

It is a custom in many countries that the diploma of admission into the Sodality is framed and affixed in the room of the Sodalist as a constant reminder of the great privilege and the sacred obligations entailed in membership in this important organization.

Feasts of Mary

Of the five major feasts of the Blessed Virgin, only two are holy days of obligation (the Assumption and the Immaculate Conception). The other three, however, might very well be also kept with some fitting celebration, especially since they commemorate such important events in the lives of Jesus and Mary: the Purification (February 2), the Annunciation

(March 25) and the Nativity of Mary (September 8).

On these three feasts, at least some members of the family could attend the Holy Sacrifice, if possible. Some devotional and religious celebration might be added to the regular daily routine. One custom which is kept in many families is the reading before dinner or at the family devotion in the evening of the Gospel from the Mass of the day.

Those who attend Mass on the feast of the *Purification* (Candlemas) should bring home to the family one or two of the blessed candles to keep in the house and burn on special occasions, such as feast days, during novenas, in sickness and in time of danger.

The feast of the *Annunciation* is a traditional day of prayer among farmers to obtain, through Mary's intercession, blessing upon the spring planting. Perhaps our Catholic families could offer some prayers for the same intention on this day. It would make the children realize how much we depend on nature for our basic needs of the body and teach them the lesson to pray for the temporal welfare, not only of their family and friends, but of all the people in the country.

The feast of the *Assumption* is the oldest and, in a sense, the greatest holyday of Mary. We celebrate not only her passing from this world, but also her glorious Assumption, with body and soul, into eternal bliss, and her "crowning" in Heaven, that is, her elevation to the dignity of Queen over all creatures. For every Catholic family it should be a day of great devotion and joy. Many nationalities, especially the Italian and Portuguese people, celebrate this day with processions and festivities; the ships of fishing fleets are solemnly blessed, and people present each other with fruit or flowers in honor of Mary.

On the feast of Our Lady's *Nativity,* we celebrate her earthly birthday, which was different from ours in that she was born without Original Sin. I know a home where the smaller children decorate the family shrine (which bears Mary's statue) on this day with flowers and evergreens after breakfast, and then sing "Happy Birthday" in her honor. In some places, the school children start a novena in the home on this day, to pray for Our Lady's blessing and help in the coming school year. High school and college students could easily make a similar novena on their own.

The feast of the *Immaculate Conception* reminds us that Mary was entirely free from Original Sin and that her soul was always pure and radiant with the fullness of God's grace. Coming at the start of a new ecclesiastical year, this feast might serve as the first great day of a devout and conscious preparation for Christmas. For parents, it might present a fitting occasion to encourage the children in praying to the Blessed Virgin for help against temptations and for her protection against the dangers of bad company—a very real danger in our times.

-24-

ALL SAINTS DAY, ALL SOULS DAY, HALLOWEEN

ALL SAINTS DAY

The feast of All Saints was established by the Church because a very large number of martyrs and other Saints could not be accorded the honor of individual celebrations, since the days of the year would not suffice. Therefore, as the Prayer of the Mass states, "we venerate the merits of all the Saints by this one celebration." There is another reason for the feast. Pope Urban IV mentioned it in the following words: "Any negligence, omission and irreverence committed in the celebration of the Saints' feasts throughout the year is to be atoned for by the faithful, and thus due honor may still be offered these Saints." (Pope Urban IV, *Decretale Si Dominum*).

It might be pointed out that from the very beginning the commemoration of All Saints Day included also, in a special way, the Blessed Virgin. When Pope Boniface IV, in 615, dedicated the former pagan temple of the Pantheon in Rome as a church, he called it the church of the "Blessed Virgin Mary and all the Martyrs." Thus All Saints Day is really a great feast day of Mary, too.

Perhaps this could be the day to acquaint the children with the Litany of the Saints, by saying it together at the family devotion or by encouraging the older ones to recite it on their own. They should become aware of the groupings of Saints under collective invocations ("All holy patriarchs and prophets," etc.). Thus they will understand that the Church does not try to mention all Saints individually, but only chose a few representatives of each group. The second part of the litany will teach the children how to pray for the main needs, both temporal and spiritual, of the whole Christian world.

It was, and still is, a general custom to serve special "All Saints" pastry on this day. Usually it is made of sweet dough, with eggs, milk and raisins, and shaped in different forms and sizes according to tradition in various places. Perhaps families in this country could make such All Saints cakes, too. It does not matter what kind of mix or shape is used, as long as it is a distinctive feature of the feast and will remain associated with All Saints Day in the minds of the children.

ALL SOULS DAY

The commemoration of all the Holy Souls in Purgatory was introduced by St. Odilo, abbot of Cluny, about the year 1000. He prescribed that all the monks of his Benedictine congregation should offer the Holy Sacrifice and say prayers for the suffering souls every year on November 2. The popes in Rome gladly accepted this wonderful and charitable thought and extended the celebration to the whole Church. Since then, we do not only pray for the Holy Souls throughout the year, but have a special day devoted to their prayerful memory. Pope Benedict XV, in 1915, allowed all priests to say three Masses on All Souls Day, so our dear departed ones will receive greater help from us and an abundance of mercy from God.

The main religious exercise we can perform on All Souls Day is, of course, to attend the Holy Sacrifice and offer it for the departed ones. That is why an ancient custom in many countries demands that at least one member of every family go to church and Mass. It is also a custom to say the Rosary or other prayers at home for the Holy Souls, and to offer up some acts of charity for them.

On the afternoon of All Saints Day, and during the whole of All Souls Day, many Catholics go to the cemeteries to pray at the graves of their dear departed. They decorate the tombs with lights and lanterns, and all the graves are adorned with flowers.

Catholic parents might prudently explain to their children that we should not only pray *for* the Holy Souls, to help *them,* but that we may also pray *to* them for their intercession, to help *us.* It is a fact often mentioned among sincere Catholics that the Holy Souls invariably show their great power of intercession by unusual and surprising answers to our petitions. Not only in big and serious matters, but even in little things they seem anxious to help us, if only we turn to them in great confidence.

HALLOWEEN

Although the name of this tradition is taken from the great Christian feast (All Hallows' Eve), the observance of Halloween pranks, masquerading, "trick or treat" and similar features are not based on any religious background nor connected with any Christian meaning. This practice has come down to us from the demon lore of the ancient Druids.

In a Catholic home, therefore, the participation of the children in such Halloween activities should not be explained as a part of the Christian feast, because such explanations would be erroneous. It is an ancient popular custom from pagan times which has never been associated with Christian meanings. Let the children enjoy their Halloween festival, if you wish, but apart from it direct their minds to the fact that this evening is primarily a time of preparation for the great feast of All Saints, and that after the Halloween frolics they should turn their minds to God in a devout evening prayer, and greet all the heroes of God on the eve of their feast.*

---

*In recent years there has grown up the fine custom of holding an All Saints Day party on Halloween evening as a replacement for the usual Halloween observances. At this party each child dresses in costume as a particular Saint. —*Publisher,* 1998.

THANKSGIVING

We have no liturgical feast of thanksgiving on any one day of the year because the highest act of thanksgiving to God is performed daily in the Holy Sacrifice. Thus in the Catholic Church every day is "Thanksgiving Day."

However, the people wanted to show their special gratitude to God by some popular celebration at the happy conclusion of the annual harvest, and so they started the custom in medieval times of keeping a great feast on the day of St. Martin (November 11). They went to Mass in the morning, then had a big dinner at noon, at which they ate a roast goose (Martin's goose) and drank wine from the first lot of the new grape harvest (Martin's love).

When the Pilgrims came to America, they brought this ancient Christian custom with them. On their first Thanksgiving, they looked for the traditional geese. In fact, they caught some wild geese, but not enough for all. So they used other birds as well, ducks and wild turkeys. This was the beginning of the American custom of eating turkey on Thanksgiving Day. The Pilgrims also kept the custom of drinking wine which was made from the first pressing of the new grape harvest.

Our Thanksgiving Day, therefore, is based on an ancient tradition of Christianity. As the people did in the old times, so Catholic families today might attend the Holy Sacrifice on Thanksgiving Day. We have great and good reasons to thank God not only for all His temporal and spiritual blessings given to our families, but also in a special way for the fact that our people acknowledge His goodness by thanking Him on one special day of the year in the name of the entire nation. It might be a fitting suggestion to say an extra prayer before dinner on Thanksgiving Day, a small but sincere prayer, in the name of all those families who do not thank God, even on this day.

–26–

SOME FEASTS OF SAINTS

Every Catholic family will have a particular devotion to various Saints whom they have come to know, love and invoke in a special way. The grace of God inspires us to choose such Saints according to our needs and inclinations. It is a sign of healthy religious life if a family venerates and celebrates its "own" favorite Saints.

There are a few Saints, however, who through their position or through some special custom connected with their feasts have become favorite patrons and intercessors for Christians. We present here a few short paragraphs about the feasts of such "general patrons" whose celebration is recommended to Catholic families.

St. Blaise (February 3)

He was a bishop in Armenia and suffered martyrdom for Christ in the persecution of the Emperor Diocletian at the beginning of the fourth century. The legends tell us that he had been a physician before he became bishop and that he miraculously cured a little boy who nearly died of a fishbone in his throat.

St. Blaise is invoked as a great helper in sickness and pain, but especially against evils of the throat. The best-known sacramental in his honor is the "Blessing of Throats" with candles. The priest holds the crossed candles against the head or throat of the person and says: "Through the intercession of St. Blaise, bishop and martyr, may God deliver you from ailments of the throat and from every other evil. In the name of the Father, and of the Son, and of the Holy Ghost. Amen."

St. Joseph (March 19)

The foster-father of Our Lord is one of the most powerful helpers and intercessors at the throne of God. Catholics everywhere love him and pray to him in all their needs. As the Bible quotes the words of the Pharao about Joseph of Egypt (*Gen.* 41:55), so the Church today admonishes us to invoke the holy spouse of the Blessed Virgin Mary: "Go to Joseph!" Filled with affection, love and confidence, the faithful turn to him in all their temporal and spiritual worries. He is patron of Christian families and homes, of tradesmen and workers. (That is why we now have the feast of "St. Joseph the Worker"—May 1.) For our spiritual lives, his patronage of purity, prayer, recollection and humility is a powerful example and help. He is also the heavenly patron of engaged couples, of those who suffer temporal distress (poverty, need of position, domestic troubles, sickness, financial worries, etc.), and patron of a happy death.

Every Catholic child should receive from his parents, at an early age, the precious inheritance of a great devotion to St. Joseph. His feast day should be celebrated in every home with appropriate features of prayer and festivity.

St. Anthony of Padua (June 13)

This famous and lovable Saint was a native of Lisbon. He entered the Franciscan Order and died, still young, at Padua in Italy (1231). His life and legend inspired the faithful everywhere with confidence and devotion. He is a special patron of the poor, of girls who look for a husband, of married women and of Christian soldiers fighting against enemies of the Faith. His best-known patronage, however, is the power of restoring all kinds of lost things. In great and little matters, millions of people—Catholics and non-

Catholics—constantly pray to him to help them find things they have mislaid or lost.

St. John the Baptist (June 24)

He was highly honored throughout the Church from the very beginning. Since he was "filled with the Holy Ghost even from his mother's womb" (*Luke* 1:15), he was born with sanctifying grace in his soul; therefore, the Church now celebrates his earthly birthday. So great was the rank of his feast in the Middle Ages that three Masses were celebrated, just as on Christmas.

The holy Baptist is patron of tailors (because he made his own garments in the desert), of shepherds (because he spoke of the "Lamb of God") and of masons (because he exhorted people to build the "road of the Lord"). Above all, however, he is an example and patron of self-denial and of doing your duty, even if it hurts. This brings the Saint very close to children, who have to learn this very lesson and will greatly appreciate his help.

Sts. Peter and Paul (June 29)

According to ancient tradition, these two Apostles were put to death by the Emperor Nero. St. Peter died by crucifixion in the public amphitheater at the Vatican hill; St. Paul was beheaded outside the city. Their feast was observed as a holyday of obligation from the fifth century on. It has remained so through all the centuries since. (In the United States the faithful are dispensed from the law of attending Mass and of holyday rest).

The feast of Sts. Peter and Paul might be used by parents to explain to their children the great office of the Apostles, the primacy of St. Peter and the dignity and spiritual power of the Holy Father in Rome. Pictures of St. Peter's Cathedral and of the Vatican might be shown to them to make them realize that the greatest church of Christianity is also the tomb-monument of the poor fisherman whom Our Lord chose to be the first leader of His kingdom on earth. Seeing pictures of the Vatican and of the apartment windows of the Holy Father, the children also will understand how the successor of St. Peter lives and works close to the tomb of the holy Apostle who was the first Pope.

St. Christopher (July 25)

Only the name of this Saint and the fact of his martyrdom are known. He is said to have died in Palestine or Lebanon. But very early, many legends were told about him, especially the story of how he was a giant and one day carried Our Lord in the appearance of a little Child across a deep river. He almost broke down under the increasing weight of this Child, until he was finally told that he had carried the Lord of Heaven and earth on his shoulders.

St. Christopher was widely venerated as a patron against sudden death. In past centuries people prayed to him when epidemics broke out and many died within the day. In modern times his help and protection are asked against traffic accidents, which kill almost as many people as the epidemics did in ancient times.

This is the reason why St. Christopher's medals are put in automobiles or carried by the faithful when they travel. On the Saint's feast day, a special blessing of cars may be obtained. However, a new automobile may be blessed any day of the year. Parents who secure the ministry of a priest in blessing their car should try to make this ceremony somewhat impressive and have all their children witness it.

St. Ann (July 26)

The name of St. Ann is not mentioned in the Bible. It was only in some legendary books of the early Christians that the names of Mary's parents were given as Joachim and Anna. The Crusaders brought the legends and the names to

Europe, and from that time on a great popular veneration of St. Ann has spread into all parts of the Christian world.

The Grandmother of Jesus soon became a special patron of married women, and for childless couples a powerful intercessor in obtaining children. But she is also invoked everywhere as one of the great helpers in various needs of body and soul.

From the eighteenth century on, her name, which means "grace," was used more and more as a favorite name for girls. Even today, many parents give their daughters the name "Ann," at least as a middle name (Mary Ann, Marianne, Marian, Joanne, Lillian, Martha Ann, Patricia Ann, Louise Ann, etc.). This is a beautiful custom which deserves to be highly recommended.

FEAST OF THE GUARDIAN ANGELS (OCTOBER 2)

The Bible often speaks of Angels helping humans, bringing God's messages to them and protecting them in dangers. Of little children we have the additional assurance through Our Lord's own words: "Their angels in heaven always see the face of my Father in heaven." (*Matt.* 18:10).

The veneration of the Guardian Angels is one of the most appealing and consoling practices in a Christian family. At the earliest possible time, children should learn from mother about their Guardian Angel and be taught to invoke him every day. Besides, parents themselves should daily pray to the Guardian Angels of their little ones. Since God gave us these heavenly spirits as personal helpers and loving friends, how could we neglect them in our religious lives?

The feast of the Guardian Angels certainly should be a special day of festive joy in every Catholic family. Because of Our Lord's words, little children should be accorded some extra celebration, and a simple but inspiring devotion might be held with them before the family shrine.

A family of my acquaintance has introduced the custom that the children will on their own, without having to be reminded, go to their room and say a little prayer of thanksgiving to their Guardian Angel whenever they have escaped from harm and danger in their daily play and activities. It is truly remarkable how often such incidents occur, that a child narrowly escapes some serious injury, "as if someone had quickly guided his movements" (these are the words of a friend of mine who is father of nine children).

PRAYER

O God, through the intercession of the Blessed Virgin Mary, grant Thy blessing and grace, that this little booklet may do some good in Thy holy kingdom and help our families "to celebrate our earthly feasts in such a way that thereby we may attain to the joys of eternity."*

---

*See the Collect (Prayer) of Wednesday in Easter Week.

–Appendix 1–
(Added by the Publisher, 1998.)

POPULAR SAINTS' NAMES FOR BAPTISM AND CONFIRMATION

MASCULINE

Albert	Francis	Lawrence	Paul
Andrew	George	Leonard	Peter
Anthony	Gerard	Louis	Philip
Augustine	Gregory	Luke	Raymond
Benedict	Henry	Marcel	Richard
Bernard	Hugh	Mark	Robert
Charles	Ignatius	Martin	Sebastian
Christopher	James	Matthew	Stephen
Damien	Jerome	Matthias	Thomas
Daniel	John	Michael	Timothy
David	Joseph	Nathaniel	Vincent
Dominic	Jude	Nicholas	William
Edward	Justin	Patrick	Xavier

FEMININE

Agnes	Dorothy	Josefa	Nicole
Andrea	Elizabeth	Josephine	Patricia
Angela	Frances	Juanita	Paula
Ann, Anne	Gabriella	Julia, Julie	Philomena
Barbara	Gemma	Louise	Priscilla
Bernadette	Genevieve	Lucia	Rita
Bridget	Georgia	Madeleine	Roberta
Catherine	Gertrude	Margaret	Rose
Cecilia	Helen	Martha	Teresa
Christine	Irene	Martina	Therese
Clare	Jane	Mary, Marie	Ursula
Colette	Jean, Jeanne	Michelle	Veronica
Danielle	Joan	Monica	Zita

THE ADVENT WREATH

Father: Our help is in the name of the Lord.

All: Who hath made Heaven and earth.

Father: Let us pray. O God, by Whose word all things are sanctified, pour forth Thy blessing upon this wreath, and grant that we who use it may prepare our hearts for the coming of Christ and may receive from Thee abundant graces. Through Christ our Lord.

All: Amen.

He then sprinkles the wreath with holy water.

The following prayers are said during each week before the evening meal.

THE FIRST WEEK

The first purple candle is lighted by the youngest child and left burning during the evening meal.

Father: O Lord, stir up Thy power, we beg Thee, and come, that by Thy protection we may deserve to be rescued from the threatening dangers of our sins and be saved by Thy deliverance. Through Christ our Lord.

All: Amen.

THE SECOND WEEK

The first and second purple candles are lighted by the oldest child during this week.

Father: O Lord, stir up our hearts that we may prepare the ways of Thine only begotten Son, that through His coming we may be made worthy to serve Thee with purified minds. Through Christ our Lord.

All: Amen.

THE THIRD WEEK

The first two purple candles and the pink candle are lighted by the mother during this week.

Father: O Lord, we beseech Thee, incline Thine ear to our prayers and enlighten the darkness of our minds by the grace of Thy visitation. Through Christ our Lord.

All: Amen.

THE FOURTH WEEK

All four candles are lighted by the father during this week.

Father: O Lord, we beseech Thee, stir up Thy power and come; and with great might deliver us, that with the help of Thy grace, Thy merciful forgiveness may hasten what our sins impede. Through Christ our Lord.

All: Amen.

–Appendix 3–

(Added by the Publisher, 1998.)

THE "O ANTIPHONS"

(Greater Antiphons)

December 17

O WISDOM, Who didst come out of the mouth of the Most High, reaching from end to end and ordering all things mightily and sweetly: come and teach us the way of prudence.

December 18

O ADONAI, and Leader of the house of Israel, Who didst appear to Moses in the flame of the burning bush, and didst give unto him the Law on Sinai: come and with an outstretched arm redeem us.

December 19

O ROOT OF JESSE, Who dost stand for an ensign of the people, before Whom kings shall keep silence, and unto Whom the Gentiles shall make their supplication: come to deliver us, and tarry not.

December 20

O KEY OF DAVID and Sceptre of the house of Israel, Who dost open and no man doth shut, Who dost shut and no man doth open, come and bring forth from his prison-house the captive that sitteth in darkness and in the shadow of death.

DECEMBER 21

O DAWN OF THE EAST, Brightness of the Light Eternal and Sun of Justice, come and enlighten them that sit in darkness and in the shadow of death.

DECEMBER 22

O KING OF THE GENTILES and the Desired of them, Thou Cornerstone that dost make both one, come and deliver man, whom Thou didst form out of the dust of the earth.

DECEMBER 23

O EMMANUEL, our King and Lawgiver, the Expected of the Nations and their Saviour, come to save us, O Lord our God.

–Appendix 4–

(Added by the Publisher, 1998. Requirements taken from the official Enchiridion of Indulgences, *1969.)*

HOW TO GAIN A PLENARY INDULGENCE

An indulgence is the remission of the temporal punishment due to be suffered for sins that have already been forgiven. This punishment must be suffered either on earth or in Purgatory. A *Partial Indulgence* remits part of the temporal punishment due; a *Plenary Indulgence* remits all the temporal punishment due. Indulgences can always be offered for the Poor Souls in Purgatory, rather than for ourselves; however, indulgences offered for the Poor Souls are efficacious by way of *suffrage,* that is, depending on God's decision, since the Church on earth does not have jurisdiction over the souls in Purgatory.

A Catholic, being in the state of grace, can gain a *Plenary Indulgence* by many different prayers and works of piety, but these four are worthy of special mention:

1. Making a **visit to the Blessed Sacrament** to adore It for at least one half hour.

2. Spending at least one half hour **reading Sacred Scripture,** as spiritual reading, with the veneration due to the Word of God.

3. **Making the Way of the Cross.** This includes walking from Station to Station. (At publicly held Stations, if this cannot be done in an orderly way, at least the leader must move from Station to Station.) No specific prayers are required, but devout meditation on the Passion and Death of

Our Lord is required (though not necessarily on the individual Stations).

4. **Recitation of the Rosary** (of at least 5 decades), with devout meditation on the Mysteries in addition to the vocal recitation, in a church, family group, religious community or pious association.

A *Plenary Indulgence* applicable only to the souls in Purgatory is granted to the faithful who on **All Souls' Day** (November 2) piously visit a Catholic church and there recite one Our Father and the Creed.*

ADDITIONAL REQUIREMENTS FOR GAINING A PLENARY INDULGENCE

In addition to performing the specified work, these three conditions are required:

1. Confession;
2. Holy Communion;
3. Prayer for the Holy Father's intentions (one Our Father and one Hail Mary suffice).

The three conditions may be fulfilled several days before or after the performance of the prescribed work; it is, however, fitting that Communion be received and the prayer for the intention of the Holy Father be recited on the same day the work is performed.

In addition, in order to gain a Plenary Indulgence a person's mind and heart must be free from all attachment to sin, even venial sin. If one tries to gain a Plenary Indulgence but fails to fulfill all the conditions, he obtains a partial indulgence. Only one Plenary Indulgence may be gained per day (except at "the moment of death").

---

*Enchiridion of Indulgences (1969), Grant 67, which includes this notice: "The above indulgence is contained in the Apostolic Constitution *The Doctrine of Indulgences,* Norm 15, with account being taken of proposals made to the Sacred Penitentiary in the meantime."

If we generously offer indulgences for the Holy Souls in Purgatory, we may hope to obtain relief or release for many of them, in accord with God's holy will. In gratitude they may well obtain for us many great favors.

Approval for "How to Gain a Plenary Indulgence":

Nihil Obstat:

    Reverend Monsignor Charles W. McNamee, S.T.L., J.C.L.
    Censor Librorum

Imprimatur:

    ✝Most Reverend Thomas G. Doran, D.D., J.C.D.
    Bishop of Rockford
    March 31, 1998

The *Nihil Obstat* and *Imprimatur* are official declarations that a book or pamphlet is free from doctrinal or moral error. No implications are contained there that those who have granted the *Nihil Obstat* or *Imprimatur* agree with the contents, opinions or statements expressed.

If you have enjoyed this book, consider making your next selection from among the following . . .

Prices subject to change.

Prices subject to change.

At your Bookdealer or direct from the Publisher.
Call Toll-Free 1-800-437-5876.

Prices subject to change.